CRIME IN THE REPUBLIC OF IRELAND: STATISTICAL TRENDS AND THEIR INTERPRETATION

GW00703372

Copies of this paper may be obtained from The Economic and Social Research Institute (Limited Company No. 18269). Registered Office: 4 Burlington Road, Dublin 4.

Price IR£5.50

(Special rate for Students IR£2.75)

David B. Rottman is a Research Officer at
The Economic and Social Research Institute.
The paper has been accepted for publication
by the Institute, which is not responsible for
either the content, or the views expressed
therein.

CRIME IN THE REPUBLIC OF IRELAND: STATISTICAL TRENDS AND THEIR INTERPRETATION

DAVID B. ROTTMAN

DUBLIN, 1980

ISBN 0 7070 0036 X

Acknowledgements

I wish to acknowledge the assistance, encouragement, and advice that I received from various individuals and groups.

Earlier versions of the paper benefited from the critical comments of my ESRI colleagues, especially those of Damian Hannan, Brendan Whelan, and Sue Scott, and from those provided by Ciaran McCullagh (University College, Cork), Leo Carroll (University of Rhode Island), and the external referee.

I received considerable assistance in assembling and analysing the data for the paper from Felix O'Regan and Pádraig Ó Seaghdha. The material contained in Chapter 6 is based, in part, on work undertaken jointly with P. Ó Seaghdha.

The Department of Justice's willingness to provide me with unpublished statistics on the distribution of offences by type of area and on homicides made possible the analyses in Chapters 5 and 6. I am grateful for that cooperation and for the assistance of the members of the Garda Siochana who collated the material I had requested.

All interpretations found in the paper are entirely my responsibility, as are all errors and inaccuracies.

CONTENTS

		Page
General Summary		1

Chapter

1	Introduction: The Problem of Crime	8
2	Crime and Social Change: Perspectives and Expectations	15
3	Data Sources: Availability and Adequacy	36
4	National Level Crime Trends: Description and Analysis.	50
5	Urban–Rural Differences in Crime Trends	83
6	Homicide and Social Change	117
7	Conclusions and Implications	141
	References	150

LIST OF TABLES

Table		Page
1	National, County Dublin, and Dublin Urban Area Populations at each Census from 1926 to 1971	30
2	Personnel and Budget of the Garda Siochana, 1951–75	65
3	National Detection Rates, 1951–75	67
4	Variance in Crime Indicators Attributable to Trend: Linear and Semi-Logarithmic Regressions	69
5	Intercorrelations among Crime Indicators, by Time-Period	72
6	Change Indices for 1951–75: Personal Expenditure on Consumer Goods, Value of Property Stolen in Burglary, and the Ratio of Property Value to Personal Expenditure	76
7	The Regression of Offence Indicators on Economic Conditions and Trend, 1955–75	80
8	The Average Value of Property Stolen in Burglaries, by Area-Type	88
9	Detection Rates for Burglary, by Area-Type	90
10	Detection Rates for Larceny from Motor Vehicles, by Area-Type	95
11	Larceny of Motor Vehicles per 10,000 Registered Vehicles, by Area-Type	98
12	Detection Rates for Larceny of Motor Vehicles, by Area-Type	98
13	Detection Rates for Larceny of Pedal Cycles, by Area-Type	100
14	Detection Rates for Robbery, by Area-Type	103
15	Incidence of Armed Roberies: 1964–75	103
16	Detection Rates for Indictable Assaults, by Area-Type	109
17	Intercorrelations Among Offence Indicators, by Area-Type, 1964–75	111
18	Correlations Among Area Offence Levels: 1964–75	114
19	Incidence of Homicide and Infanticide, 1951–75.	120
20	Expected and Observed Distributions of Homicides: Urban/Rural and Regional Classifications	130

		Page
21	Victim/Offender Relationships: 1950s and 1970s	131
22	Sex of Offender by Sex of Victim: 1950s and 1970s	131
23	Average Ages of Victims and Offenders: 1950s and 1970s	133
24	Regional Variation in Victim Age: Ratios of Average Victim and Average Population Ages	134
25	Regression Results: Additive Effects (Metric Coefficients) on the Ages of Offenders: 1950s and 1970s	135
26	Regression Results: Additive Effects (Metric Coefficients) on the Ages of Victims: 1950s and 1970s	138

LIST OF FIGURES

Figure		*Page*
1	National Trends for Housebreaking and for Shop-breaking, 1951–1975	52
2	Average Value of Property Stolen in Burglaries (in constant, 1953, prices) 1951–1975	54
3	The Total Value of Property Stolen in Burglaries (in £000s), 1951–1975	56
4	National Trends for Motor Vehicle Larceny and for Receiving Stolen Property, 1951–1975	58
5	National Trends for Larceny From Motor Vehicles and for Pedal Cycle Larceny, 1951–1975	59
6	National Trends for Assault and for Robbery, 1951–1975	62
7	Availability of Motor Vehicles and Motor Vehicle Larcenies, 1951–1975	78
8	Number of Recorded Burglaries, by Area-Type	87
9	Number of Recorded Larcenies From Unattended Vehicles, by Area-Type	92

10 Larcenies From Unattended Vehicles per 1,000 Registered Vehicles, by Area-Type   94

11 Number of Recorded Larcenies of Motor Vehicles, by Area-Type   96

12 Number of Recorded Larcenies of Pedal Cycles, by Area-Type   99

13 Number of Recorded Robberies, by Area-Type   102

14 Number of Recorded Receiving Stolen Property Offences, by Area-Type   105

15 Number of Recorded Indictable Assaults, by Area-Type   107

General Summary

There is widespread agreement that crime in Ireland has become both more frequent and more costly in the past two decades. Crime is today a recognised social problem, its magnitude a subject of public concern and the possibilities for its amelioration a matter of public debate. The statistics which the Garda Siochana compile and publish are the only available evidence on which such discussion can be based, lifting the annual *Report on Crime* from relative obscurity to a prominence it is not really designed to hold. In newspaper coverage and in the Dáil, the annual increases, or, more rarely, decreases in the number of indictable offences are taken as a score card of garda failure and success, of disorder and public order. However, despite the interest in the problem of crime and in the crime statistics, there have been few research studies of the issues involved.

This paper is an attempt to approach those issues using the concepts and methods of the social sciences. In particular, it examines two basic, though often unstated, assumptions that underlie the discussion of crime in Ireland. The first is that the published crime statistics offer an unambiguous measure of the changes that are occurring in the level and pattern of crime. The second is that Ireland is currently re-enacting the experiences of other industrial countries, particularly the United States and Great Britain. Both assumptions have been questioned; the present study attempts to do so systematically.

There are three main objectives: (a) to evaluate the available statistical evidence on trends in the level and the pattern of crime in Ireland, selecting the most meaningful indicators from that evidence for use in the analysis; (b) to measure the changes that have taken place in the 1951–1975 period; and, most importantly, (c) to interpret those changes, offering an explanation as to why they have taken place. The three objectives are intended to form a unity, the coherence resulting from the guidance provided by the major theoretical perspectives on the relationship between social change and crime. It is argued that the most useful perspective is one that focuses on changes in the manner in which a society is organised. Such changes establish the framework within which individual and collective action become possible, including those actions that are defined as criminal.

Statistics on Crime

In comparison to what is available for most countries, the crime statistics collected and published by the Garda Siochana offer a wealth of detailed and reliable evidence. The enhanced reliability stems from the use of a consistent set of rules for classifying and counting the offences of which the gardai are

1

aware. However, over the 25 years considered, substantial changes have been introduced into those rules, necessitating caution in the use of the garda statistics. And the traditional limitations of official crime statistics — under-reporting and under-recording of the "true" level at which offences occur — have been minimised rather than eliminated.

Given the preoccupation in the study with measuring and interpreting trends, the selection of indicators from the garda crime statistics is deter-mined primarily by the confidence that can be placed in the comparisons over time: the difference between offence levels in any two years should reflect the actual rate of change in the prevalence of that offence. This does not require that the official statistics represent a full inventory of all violations of the rele-vant statutes, only that extraneous influences are minimised and act in a con-sistent manner over the time period studied.

Nine crime indicators were selected. Five represent specific offences cor-responding to major forms of property crime: housebreaking, shopbreaking, larceny of motor vehicles, robbery, and receiving stolen property. Larceny from motor vehicles and pedal cycle larceny were also included, as both in-dicators share with larceny of motor vehicles a connection with a specific form of property. The average value of the property stolen in burglary (housebreaking and shopbreaking combined) was used as a measure of the changing seriousness of financial loss from property crime. It is possible for property crime to become more frequent, but the amount misappropriated per offence to remain unchanged. In addition to the eight indicators relating to property crime, the level of indictable assault is included as a guide to changes in offences against persons.

The published garda statistics were supplemented for this study in two basic ways. First, the changes in the nine indicators were examined separate-ly for each of three types of area: the Dublin Metropolitan Area, the next four largest cities combined (Cork, Galway, Limerick and Waterford), and the remainder of the country, which with some misgivings is termed the non-urban areas. Second, the files maintained by the gardai on homicides during the 1951–1975 period were used to move beyond the simple enumeration of known offences that forms the bulk of the analysis. Information was collected on the location and the circumstances, including the characteristics of the in-dividuals involved, in the 169 homicides recorded in two periods: the 1950s and 1970/74.

The analysis of the nine indicators involved a series of comparisons. At the national level, the major general forms of property crime were compared with those directed at specific forms of property, and property crime was con-trasted with the trends found for assault and homicide. In doing so, both the magnitude of the overall increase registered and the trend by which that increase occurred were considered. There are three basic forms that trends in crime statistics can assume: (a) constant growth at an invariant rate; (b) a curvilinear trend, in which the rate of change increases in the course of time; (c) a discontinuity in the level and pattern of crime through a structural shift, in which an abrupt break occurs, marking the end of one period and the beginning of another.

Trends in the Crime Statistics

In order to measure the changes between 1951 and 1975 in the frequency and the gravity of crime, the annual numbers of recorded offences and the average values of stolen property were assembled in sequence. The trends in the nine indicators thus revealed can be expressed both graphically through charts and statistically through regression analysis.

However expressed, the national trends for the major property offences confirm that a substantial increase has occurred in the frequency of those crimes. In 1975, there were five times as many recorded shopbreakings, six times as many housebreakings, and 29 times as many robberies as had been recorded in 1951. Larcenies of motor vehicles had increased 27-fold over those years, and larcenies from unattended vehicles, seven-fold. The frequency of other property offences evinced either a slight increase (receiving stolen property) or the absence of an upward trend (pedal cycle larceny), while the average value of property stolen in burglaries during 1975 was one and a half times greater than the average for 1951, taking inflation into account.

A substantial increase was also registered for offences against persons: the number of indictable assaults rose seven-fold over the 25 years, a trend in accord with that found for the statistics on homicide.

The basic consistency of massive increases is paralleled by a consistent sequencing of the upward trends. For all offences except assault and pedal cycle larceny, the bulk of the growth in crime levels occurred subsequent to 1964. Throughout the 1950s and continuing into the early 1960s, the various indicators record cyclical fluctuations around an essentially horizontal trend line. Few sustained increases were evident in the initial 13 years of the series. In all property offence indicators except that of pedal cycle larceny, a dramatic and apparently permanent break with that pattern occurs around 1964. Henceforth, the pace of increase was rapid, though for some indicators it tapered off by 1973 or 1974. A watershed clearly divides the trends in those indicators; the proper statistical specification for what took place is that of a structural break: what occurred after 1964 had no precedent in the earlier years.

Thus, if the nine crime indicators and the homicide data are indeed accurate guides to what took place between 1951 and 1975, a substantial increase in the level of crime cannot be gainsaid. Not only did the numbers of recorded offences grow dramatically, but also a watershed can be identified in the mid-1960s, marking a decisive break with the pattern of essentially stable offence levels that obtained throughout the 1950s and early 1960s. Crime did indeed become a more acute social problem. However, there is no basis for asserting that the pattern of property crime, and particularly its seriousness, experienced a comparable transformation. Crime may be more prevalent today, but the available evidence argues against an image of crime becoming more efficient and sophisticated in its execution – or more profitable.

In our imagery of crime, dangerous places are urban places. Using the data on the distribution of offences among area-types over the 1964–75 period, it was possible to test the accuracy of that perception.

Overall, the evidence argues for the essential similarity in the trends for the three types of area. Only for homicide, housebreaking and larceny from vehicles did urban trends dominate the upward movement in the crime statistics found at the national level. In all other instances, the non-urban areas recorded increases equivalent or in excess of those found in the four-cities, and for several indicators the non-urban trends were greater than those found in Dublin. Urban offence levels are higher than those found in rural areas, and that difference is somewhat accentuated over the 12 years, but the upward trend for assault and for major property offences are clear in all areas. Certainly the presence of substantial increases in crime levels outside of the major cities is clear. Such consistency in urban and non-urban trends is not in accord with the basic assumptions of most discussions of crime in Ireland today. The theme of similarity across types of areas is further highlighted by the consistency in the sequencing of large increments over the 12 year period.

On the basis of the data on homicide, it can be concluded that the contexts of interpersonal violence changed markedly over those years. Homicides in the 1950s were distributed evenly among urban and rural areas and among the regions, with a distinct tendency for homicides within families to predominate. By the 1970s, a clear urban focus for homicides had emerged; the increased prevalence can be attributed entirely to the cities. Moreover, since rural homicide remained essentially unchanged over the 25 years, the changing pattern of homicide – with the diminution of the importance of family homicide and the corresponding increasing proportion of homicides that involve strangers – occurred in the urban centres.

Social Change and Crime: An Interpretation

A belief that rising crime rates represent one cost a society incurs for becoming modern, industrial, and affluent is understandable given the experiences of most countries over this century. But a sceptical view of the applicability of those experiences to Ireland is the most sensible point of departure for any interpretation of recent Irish crime trends.

There are two general perspectives within sociology for explaining why social change should be linked to an increased level of crime and an altered pattern of crime. One perspective adopts the argument that all change, whatever the specific form it assumes, potentially disrupts the manner in which people live and think. By removing people from restraints and controls, as well as from the familiar, change generates an increased propensity toward crime. Such an approach, which is usually termed a social disorganisation perspective, highlights the universal aspects of the process of modernisation: the growth of cities, industrial development, and affluence. A second perspective focuses on the specific manner in which the patterning of social life becomes altered in the course of change. It is not change *per se*, but the restructuring of details of ordinary lives that creates conditions conducive to a changing level and pattern of crime. Where an explanation is sought on the basis of a changing structure of opportunities and possibilities, the label structural perspective should be used.

When national level trends covering the years 1951 to 1975 were examined, the extent of the transformation that occurred in the mid-1960s emerged clearly. For seven of the eight property offence indicators, for the interrelationships among the indicators, and for the relationships the indicators have with measures of property availability and of economic conditions, the mid-1960s marks a watershed. The pattern of offence levels and of offence characteristics that had prevailed for several decades came to a conclusion around 1963, and was replaced by a new pattern. It seems reasonable to associate the emergent pattern with changes in Irish social structure that began in the late 1950s: the increase in crime was one offshoot of the adjustments being made to deep-seated structural change. The nature of the evidence precludes rejection of social disorganisation arguments, but it can be concluded that their applicability to Ireland is limited.

Urban/rural differences are also relevant to an evaluation of the usefulness of social disorganisation and structural perspectives. Had recent trends been such as to create marked disparities between types of areas, then social disorganisation explanations would appear appropriate. Such disparities were not marked, and while this does not in itself affirm the appropriateness of structural explanations, it does suggest that the latter approach is the more promising. For Ireland, a single transformation could be identified, largely ignoring boundaries between city and countryside, that between 1964 and 1975 significantly increased the level of crime, and, to a much lesser extent, altered the manner in which criminal activity is carried out.

Taken together, the national and the urban/rural trends are evidence of a substantial transformation in the level and pattern of Irish crime, a transformation that was pervasive to the society generally. The consistency among the nine indicators is marked; given the variety of offences involved and the length of the time-period studied, it is remarkable. A watershed was reached, a departure from the level and pattern that had obtained since the early 1950s. Such consistencies support, by and large, the assertion that recent changes in Irish crime arose as responses to the specific social structural changes that began around 1960. The comparisons undertaken between types of offences and types of areas do not provide convincing evidence for a view that crime was but one manifestation of a growing disorganisation within the society.

What specific components of structural change in Ireland are implicated in the new level and pattern of crime that emerged after the mid-1960s? Only a partial answer emerges from this paper. The strongest support for a connection between structural change and crime was found for those offences in which the amount and the distribution of the property "at risk" changed most dramatically over the 25 years. Trends in the availability of property are related to those for offence levels and offence seriousness in the manner suggested by the structural perspective. While the evidence is persuasive, it is not definitive; however, there is certainly ample justification for further research along the lines advocated in the paper. The results from the analysis of the impact of economic conditions on crime was more definitive, though negative: the cyclical changes in economic conditions during the 1950s, 1960s, and 1970s are but slightly related to the level of crime, and cannot have engineered the "break" that occurred in the mid-1960s.

The contrast between the social disorganisation and the structural perspectives can be made too emphatic. Both associate substantial changes in a social structure with a movement toward a higher incidence of crime. If preference is given to the structural approach, it is because it directs attention toward what is most important: the suddenness, rapidity, and pervasiveness of industrialisation in Ireland, a process that occurred far more recently here than in other western nations. Industrial development is the primary force, implicitly if not explicitly, in most attempts to explain the growth of crime. It is important particularly through its impact on urbanisation. Dublin, in contrast to most capital cities, was not a magnet for successive waves of rural migrants, and along with other Irish cities, grew gradually, largely from natural increase. Within the context of the distinctive nature of Irish industrial development and urban growth, the mid-1960 watershed is quite explicable. There is no need to equate crime with disorder or to react to the trends with despair.

Placed in the context of the social changes Ireland experienced in the late 1950s and in the 1960s, the upward trend in the crime statistics become less alarming. A transformation occurred in the extent and pattern of crime, representing an adjustment to fundamental changes in the social order. Now that the impact has largely been absorbed within the system, it is reasonable to anticipate a more restrained pace to any future increases in the crime statistics. The statistics for the late 1970s indeed support such a view. But it is again necessary to stress the limitations of the statistical evidence. Crime statistics are imprecise indices of the amount of crime in the community and can be treated as measures of year to year fluctuations only with caution. The most sensible use of crime statistics is within the framework of a perspective that is applied to a specific time-period, and that was the objective of this study.

Chapter 1

Introduction: The Problem of Crime

In the mid-1970s, the level of crime came for the first time since Independence to occupy centre stage as a topic of public concern and political debate in the Republic of Ireland. Crime became a recognised social problem, perceived as symptomatic of still graver societal ills, requiring remedial action as a matter of urgency. All this was embodied in the imagery of a war on crime, in which the gardai did battle with an enemy, a criminal element, clearly distinguishable from decent citizens. Annually, with the publication of the Garda Commissioner's *Report on Crime*, and sporadically, as questions in the Dáil produced interim tabulations, crime statistics were examined as the index of the success with which the war was being waged. Each fresh batch of statistics became translated into newspaper headlines and a renewed outcry that something be done.

This paper is a response to this sudden emergence of crime and the statistics on crime as important topics of public debate. It cannot be denied that crime today is more prevalent and inflicts greater injury and cost than was the case 15 or 20 years ago. Concern is obviously justified and an explanation is clearly called for – there would be little rationale otherwise for undertaking a major inquiry into crime as a social problem. However, it is a topic that is best approached cautiously. Crime statistics increase or decrease in response to many influences, of which actual changes in the frequency of criminal activity is but one. It is as easy to misinform as it is to inform on the basis of an uncritical reference to statistics on crime.

Caution is also required in a more general sense. Much of the discussion on crime in Ireland seeks parallels with what has been experienced in other countries. The lessons to be learned in this manner are not necessarily obvious; what occurred in the United States or in Britain earlier in this century is not an unfailing guide to what is happening, or will happen, in Ireland. The temptation to view crime as a disease that has spread in epidemic proportions around the globe since the Second World War is understandable. But it is possible, and indeed likely, that a variety of causal processes underlie the growth in crime rates that have been registered, and that the similarities among countries are at least partly illusionary. This is important, for if the antecedents to a problem can vary, so will the policy choices that will prove the most efficacious in any particular situation.

The need for caution in making inferences from crime statistics and in applying lessons learned elsewhere stimulated this study. There are three main objectives:

(1) To collate the published information on trends in crime, undertaking such adjustments as are needed to assure their relevance to the important questions being asked, and to supplement that information with new material derived specifically for this study.

(2) To analyse that information so as to have the clearest possible measure of the degree to which changes have actually occurred in the frequency and in the gravity of crime.

(3) To offer an interpretation of why those changes have taken place, with a view toward explaining what has happened and anticipating what might happen in the future.

The years covered are 1951 to 1975. During that period a clear perception developed that Ireland had changed from a society in which crime was infrequent and inconsequential to one in which a clear and growing threat exists to public order. It was indeed toward the middle of that period that the crime statistics collected by the gardai first began to increase at a rapid pace, representing a decisive break from the essentially unchanging levels of known crime that had obtained since the foundation of the state. By systematically putting together the available evidence, and by analysing and interpreting it, I hope to be able to explain the watershed which, both in the public perception and in the garda statistics, took place during the 1960s. The first step, however, will be to confirm that it did take place.

These three objectives must be met, in my opinion, if an adequate understanding of crime as a social problem is to be achieved. The statistical evidence does not speak for itself; it is valuable to the extent that it can be examined in the light of an interpretive framework that can assign a meaning to the changes that are registered. Similarly, unless the statistics on crime are adjusted and supplemented, their relevance to the issues involved in discussions of the problem will be dubious. This paper, therefore, is an attempt to bring together the materials needed for an adequate public debate on the topic of crime. Given the complexity of the issues, it cannot be, and is not intended to be, a definitive statement.

Given the availability of the annual garda crime statistics, the amount of attention given in the chapters that follow to consideration of the adequacy of the evidence may seem misplaced to some readers. We have all become accustomed, perhaps too accustomed, to the news headlines that declare an increase, or more rarely, a decrease in the amount of crime. But however they are used, crime statistics are not equivalent to a set of financial accounts, making clear statements on gain and loss. That is neither the reason nor the basis for their collection. What we know from a set of crime statistics is how the public and the police are responding to the amount of crime present in the community. Information is available on the number of occasions on which members of the public alert the gardai that a crime may have been committed and on the instances in which the gardai independently reach such a conclusion. Thus, increased police efficiency, heightened public concern over crime, or rising expectations as to what the police can, or should do, may all result in more "crime" being recorded; so may modifications introduced into the data collection procedures. Since no formal system of auditing crime statistics is followed, such modifications often go unremarked, spuriously altering the number of crimes registered.

If the first objective can be met, with the statistical evidence so adjusted as to eliminate or render manageable possible extraneous influences, then it becomes feasible to measure the amount of change in crime that has occurred in Ireland over the recent past. Both the level and the pattern of crime potentially change. By level, I refer simply to frequency. A changing pattern of crime, however, reflects the nature of criminal activity, particularly as manifested in the sophistication and organisation with which crimes are committed and the seriousness of the loss or damage. The pattern is also manifest in the relative importance of various types of crime. Public concern is clearly directed at both the prevalence and the nature of crime: in newspaper stories, political speeches, and conversation, there is a clear feeling that crime today is not only more frequent, but more sinister, more threatening. While measureing trends in the nature of crime is a more formidable problem than assessing the change in frequency, it should be undertaken to the extent possible. This paper is therefore concerned with both the level and the pattern of criminal activity in Ireland.

To provide more precise statements on the increase in crime than were hitherto available is to make a contribution. But the important objective is to interpret what occurred. If between 1951 and 1975 major changes took place in the extent and nature of crime in Ireland, presumably those changes were tied to other, more general, trends in Irish society. Assistance in defining that link can be obtained from the efforts made by criminologists to isolate the basic social processes that can be treated as causes of increasing criminal behaviour. Out of the voluminous literature devoted to the topic, expectations can be derived as to how general social change, say, in the form of urbanisation and industrialisation, transfers into a more substantial crime problem. The applicability of such expectations to the Irish situation of recent years must, as was noted, be carefully considered. It should, however, be possible to develop a perspective that can guide the interpretation of the trends that are found.

I hope the objectives of the study are now clear. The remainder of this chapter is concerned with conveying the manner in which they will be pursued. To do so requires that I describe some of the more important aspects of the approach that I adopted and outline the organisation of the paper.

The most fundamental characteristic of any approach is the answer given by the researcher to the question: What do I mean by crime? It is an embarrassingly difficult question. According to the standard dictionary definition, a crime is "an act punishable by law, as being forbidden by statute or injurious to the public welfare" (Oxford Shorter English Dictionary, 1964, p. 423). That seems reasonable, but to adopt such a definition is to cast far too wide a net – the contents that are hauled up will be so numerous and so diverse as to defy comprehension. Applied to the Irish crime statistics for 1977, that definition of crime results in 410,698 instances in which offences were brought before the courts for adjudication. If each offence represents a distinct "offender", then one out of every five citizens over age 14 was accused of committing a crime in that year.

Burglary, robbery, murder, and assault represent but a tiny fraction of the 411,000 offences. By adding petty larcenies and similar offences, the fraction merely becomes small. Eight of every ten court proceedings in the mid-1970s (83.7 per cent in 1977) arose out of legislation enacted to regulate the use made of motor vehicles by their owners. Efforts to improve society, whether through dissuading people from littering the streets and footpaths or to induce them to wear car safety belts, have increasingly come to rely on the criminal law. The inevitable result is a constant expansion in the range of behaviours that can be classified, at least formally, as criminal. But are people who break such laws criminals?

The compilers of the Oxford Dictionary acknowledge this difficulty, inserting a caveat in parentheses after their definition: "commonly used only of grave offences." This does delimit the potential field of interest somewhat, though the distinction involved is necessarily arbitrary. Also, a return to the dictionary can be avoided. A variety of approaches have been devised by legal scholars and legislators for distinguishing grave offences. In the common law tradition, within which Irish criminal law developed, four basic distinctions are made in terms of gravity (Ó Siochain, 1977, pp. 3–36).

(a) Treason: singled out as especially reprehensible;
(b) Felony: "a crime on which the law looks with a special gravity because of its seriousness and its particular offensiveness against the liberties of the people," a distinction that includes murder, forgery, embezzlement, rape, larceny (of all varieties), arson, and robbery;
(c) Misdemeanour: "the lesser social crime, lacking the offensiveness of a felony, and not capable, in the eyes of the law, of inflicting any grievous wrong on the individual or on the community," which includes assault, fraud, poaching, and public nuisance;

(d) Statutory Summary Offences: such as those regulating road traffic, in which particular actions are defined as criminal despite the absence of anything inherent – as there is held to be, say, in a burglary – that is criminal, the "crime" being created to facilitate compliance.

Such distinctions are venerable, but of limited usefulness, at least for my purpose. Certainly in terms of social injury, it is not clear that a person who breaks the summary offence against driving while intoxicated is less a danger to the public than is a shoplifter. Nor is it particularly informative to treat robbery and petty larceny as if they were of equal gravity.

This is a problem endemic to the field of criminology, not just to the present study. The traditional resolution to it has been legalistic, to argue that crime is whatever the statutes declare it to be, accepting the diversity that inevitably results. As a practical matter, studies adopting such an approach introduce arbitrary restrictions, excluding traffic offences or concentrating on a set of offence categories that are obviously serious. Clinard's (1978) study of crime in Switzerland offers a particularly relevant model of research on national crime trends that adopts a legalistic approach.

A second approach is to insist that criminology, to be scientific, must define its own subject matter. Its proponents put forward "natural properties" of actions that make them criminal, such as their social injuriousness or their violation of universal "conduct norms" (see Schwendinger and Schwendinger, 1975 for the history of this approach). The existence of a legal prohibition is irrelevant, at least in most such formulations. If this can be accomplished, the diversity that confronts criminologists will be replaced with a homogeneous phenomenon; the potential for achieving a causal explanation of crime is thereby increased.

To a considerable extent, the approach that is preferable depends on the questions that are being posed. A legalistic view of crime seems unavoidable given the terms of reference for this study. The crime statistics are generally treated as "social facts" in the Durkheimian sense – as objective phenomena in their own right. A change in those statistics does exert an influence on how people act and certainly on state policy. That some behaviours that may be injurious are excluded and others that may be innocuous are included in the level of recorded crime does not make an understanding of the statistics unimportant. They are a force in the society with real consequences.

Adopting that approach does impose limitations. In particular, it leaves open the question of whether all the statistics are equally relevant, and if not, where the boundary for inclusion is set. It is a question that will be treated in Chapter 3.

Having specified what is meant by crime in this study, some other clarifications should be made. It is in the terminology of the social sciences, a macro-level study. That is, it examines relationships and patterns at an aggregate level. The data on crime being considered are primarily at a national level. What I wish to understand are the factors underlying changes in national crime levels and patterns. The explanation will be sought in terms of the manner in which the country has changed over the same period. This is not, therefore, a study of what types of individuals commit crimes or what factors in their personalities or backgrounds are responsible. Also I wish to understand the relationships such as those that might exist between the level of crimes against property and the amount of unemployment, or that between the abundance of motor vehicles and the level of motor vehicle larceny.

It is possible to specify and examine such relationships, and to do so within a theoretical perspective, but it is to be stressed that proof will be elusive. This is not a study in which hypotheses can be definitively rejected or supported. Explanation can only take the form of plausible interpretations. I hope, however, that enough information will be provided for the reader to make his or her own assessment of exactly how plausible my interpretations and conclusions are.

Having stated the objectives for the study and outlined the approach that will be used, it remains for this introductory chapter to indicate how the paper is organised. In the six chapters that follow, the quality of the statistical evidence on crime in Ireland will be evaluated, the trends found in that evidence presented and interpreted, and, finally, a step back will be taken to obtain an overview of the evidence, indicating what conclusions can be drawn and with what certainty.

Chapter 2 provides the framework for all this. It summarises the major perspectives that criminologists have used in trying to understand long-term changes in crime. From this literature, it is possible to distil a perspective on how the broad patterns of social change – to which the labels modernisation, industrialisation, and urbanisation are generally applied – come to affect the level and nature of crime. The perspective is developed through a three part process. From the considerable body of writings that are relevant, two important ways of looking at the connection social change has to crime will be singled out and discussed in detail. Once this initial section has established a core of ideas that appear promising for my purpose, the question of their applicability to the Irish experience over the past quarter century can be addressed. Social change in Ireland does not appear to conform to the assumptions and expectations of writings generated in other countries. The implications of this distinctiveness will be considered in the third, concluding, section of the chapter, resulting, I hope, in a perspective on crime that will prove useful for Ireland.

Chapter 3 is devoted entirely to the crime statistics: what information is available for Ireland, how its usefulness and meaningfulness can be evaluated, the results of such an evaluation, and the most effective manner in which the statistical evidence can be presented. Like all social statistics, those describing crime should be used with caution. In my opinion, however, the Irish crime statistics can, if used properly, be made to speak to the major issues involved, both generally and specifically for this paper. The basis for that assertion is to be found in Chapter 3.

Chapter 4 uses the national crime statistics to chart, both graphically and statistically, the trends over the years 1951 to 1975. In later sections of the chapter, the relationship of those trends in the level and pattern of crime to changes in such features of Irish society as the abundance of property and economic conditions is measured.

In Chapter 5 the focus changes to comparisons between types of areas with a view toward understanding where the national changes were concentrated. Differences in urban and rural crime trends are of particular interest. Such differences potentially are of considerable policy relevance – in terms of the distribution of police manpower, for example – but can also help to make sense of what is occurring. Is the increase in levels of crime concentrated in urban areas? Is the pattern of crime similar in urban and in rural areas? By using a set of crime statistics collated specifically for this study, such questions can be examined for the years 1964 to 1975.

Because of the data on which they are based, Chapters 4 and 5 give us a picture of crime from which all drama and emotion have been abstracted. Aggregate statistics can inform us as to how many burglaries were recorded in a given year, the total or average value of the property thus appropriated, and the percentage of offences in which the gardai made arrests. While useful, such information is silent on the human context in which crime takes place and in how that has changed. Data on homicide, however, do not suffer from such a limitation, and in Chapter 6 the detail available on each offence is used to try and recreate, at least in part, the context in which crimes of violence occur. Specifically, homicide in the 1950s is contrasted with that in the 1970s.

Finally, Chapter 7 returns to the three objectives and summarises what has been accomplished for each.

Chapter 2
Crime and Social Change: Perspectives and Expectations

Introduction

A belief that rising crime rates somehow derive from social change is probably inevitable given the experiences of most countries over this century. A higher level of crime seems to be regarded today as one cost a society incurs for becoming industrial, modern, and affluent – the dark side of progress. This chapter surveys and evaluates the answers proposed by sociologists and criminologists to the question of how societal change comes to be reflected in the level and pattern of crime. Those answers can be grouped into two major perspectives, which will be labelled "social disorganisation" and "structural". I hope that a discussion of the main tenets of those perspectives can suggest which aspects of Irish crime trends deserve our attention and help build a framework for interpreting what those trends mean.

The question posed in this chapter is not new. While the question of why some people do, and some do not, commit violations of the criminal law may be more familiar to most readers, it is, at least within the social sciences, less venerable. Criminology as a social science began, in effect, early in the nineteenth century with the first systematic efforts to collect national crime statistics. Like statistics describing other "moral phenomena", such as suicide and alcoholism, those on crime were found to evince a characteristic rate for each country, a rate that remained remarkably consistent over time. Moreover, the relative contribution of various offence categories to that rate also appeared to be stable (Taylor *et al.*, 1973, p. 37; McClintock, 1974). To the "moral statisticans", who sought to produce a science of society based on regularities in social statistics, this indicated that social life was not of capricious origins, resting on individual propensities. Instead, they concluded that crime and like phenomena are products of a particular set of social arrangements, making explicable differences in national crime rates. When later in the century the crime statistics registered substantial increases, changing social arrangements offered the obvious explanation.

As a result, it is possible to draw for this chapter upon a literature accumulated over a century and a half. The focus, however, will be on recent formulations of the two major perspectives. Those formulations were, despite their indebtedness to earlier generations of social scientists, written in a context that is in an important sense unprecedented. At a time in which the traditional values of progress and social justice were seemingly being fulfilled to a degree never before experienced, crime was increasing at an alarming pace. It is in the light of this paradox that the post-Second World War literature on crime can be most usefully evaluated. The application to Ireland is particularly apt: just when long-standing problems of development and employment had apparently been resolved, crime came to be regarded as a major social problem.

The section that follows summarises the two perspectives and draws some conclusions as to the aspects of social change that are potentially important for understanding what has occurred in Ireland. The process of social change actually experienced by Ireland, and its correspondence to the assumptions of social disorganisation and structural perspectives, is considered in a separate section, while a concluding section evaluates the applicability of both perspectives to the Irish context.

Perspectives on Crime

Two main themes can be identified in the substantial body of writing that attempts to explain why social change should be linked to increases in the level of crime and to changes in the pattern of crime. One such theme is that all change, whatever the specific form it assumes, potentially disrupts the manner in which people live and think. Change, simply by removing people from restraints and controls, as well as from the familiar, generates an increased propensity towards crime. A second strand of thinking takes a narrower, less general, approach, arguing that what matters is the specific manner in which the patterning of social life alters. The implications of change are to be found in the details of how everyday patterns of working, family life, and leisure become altered in the course of social change.

Where emphasis is placed on the qualities of change *per se*, the term "social disorganisation perspective" will be used for purposes of this summary. A focus on the changes in the structure of social activities will be termed a "structural perspective." This distinction is made because it highlights some important issues in the study of crime trends. However, the boundary between the two perspectives can be drawn too emphatically; certainly quite a few of the authors who will be cited do not regard it as a major frontier. Both perspectives can be adapted to a situation in which prosperity and growth are accompanied by increasing crime rates. Moreover, they share a basic understanding of where an explanation must be sought: a given level and pattern of criminal activity is to be understood in terms of the prevailing social structure. If recent years have seen a fundamental change in crime, this should be attributed to the occurrence of profound economic and social change during that period.

Social structure is the concept used by sociologists to indicate the form or pattern of organisation in the social groups and institutions that constitute a society. It is a model which specifies the basic social groups and institutions, the most important positions which people hold within them, and the nature of the relationships among these positions and groups. Positions, groups, and institutions are linked by patterns of interaction that are recurrent and regularised. The concept thus refers to the pattern of interconnectedness. Social change emerges from contradictions among the components of social structure, as well as from external pressure; in sociological terms, history is constituted out of changes in social structure (Gerth and Mills, 1953; Smelser and Lipset, 1966). An illustration using the most basic of social groups, the family, may make clearer what I mean by social structure. The characteristic set of positions within families (husband-father, wife-mother, daughter-sister, son-brother) assume a particular set of relationships to one another that typifies, say, a peasant society or an industrial society. A family in a peasant society will have distinctive relationships to the economic system and political systems, markedly different from the relationships by which working class families of industrial cities will participate in those systems. In each instance, the pieces fit together in an identifiable manner. As the economic system changes, however, so will the relationships through which family members participate in it, with consequent changes in relationships within the family.

Every society manifests a social structure with distinctive attributes, but it is possible to isolate broad types of social structure and to use the resulting classification as a tool for analysis. The type relevant to the theme of this study is the advanced capitalist society. As defined by Giddens (1973, pp. 141–142) an advanced society entails "a social order in which industrialism has come to predominate in the production of marketable goods within the economy." Industrial capitalism is one variant of this basic type. A society can be termed capitalist if its economic system is predominantly organised to ensure that production is (1) directed toward producing profit for privately owned capital and (2) dependent on a market in which labour is bought and sold along with other commodities.

The social change process of interest to this paper, therefore, is that which Ireland experienced as she made the transition to become an advanced capitalist society. A variety of pathways exist through which societies can make that transition (Giddens, 1973, pp. 144–152), and the impact of social change on crime in Ireland ought to approximate most closely that which is typical of societies that had previously taken a similar path. I propose to use the main principles of social disorganisation and structural perspectives as the guide to those aspects of social structural change that are of greatest relevance to crime trends and then to consider their relevance to the Irish situation. Both perspectives, for example, emphasise the consequences of urbanisation, though with quite different views on why and how it is important. By examining Irish urbanisation in the post-1950 period, and its relationship to other aspects of social structural change, some expectations on urban/rural differences can be generated. I hope in this manner to take advantage of what has been learned in other countries about crime and social change without making facile assumptions in which Ireland's future is prefigured in the American or British present. The first step is to summarise and then evaluate the two perspectives.

The Social Disorganisation Perspective The social disorganisation perspective, which in its many formulations has had wide currency as an explanation of aggregate crime rates throughout this century, emphasises the disruption and dislocation that inevitably accompanies change. Though the content of change is therefore not usually highlighted, in effect the concern is with the processes of urbanisation and industrialisation. The intellectual roots of this approach can be found in the work of Emile Durkheim (1933); transplanted across the Atlantic, his perspective provided the inspiration for the work of several generations of American criminologists.

To Durkheim, the incidence of crime in modern societies is but one con-comitant of the alteration in the source of integration within social structures that occurs with social evolution. Consensus and homogeneity, which forged social solidarity within the communal village, become displaced by the functional interdependence that characterises the complex and segmented division of labour in industrial society. As traditional authority is eroded and an expanding division of labour results in occupational specialisation, differences between individuals become more pronounced; the strength of what is shared in experiences, attitudes, and abilities diminishes, and the possibilities for individual variation and innovation are enhanced. Such individual variation leads to deviance. The difficulties involved in maintaining a satisfactory level of moral regulation in a situation of rapid change explains, for Durkheim, the high levels of deviance characteristic of industrial society. The adequacy of the link which moral regulation provides for individuals to the larger social structure varies internally within a society. The stress and strain engendered by change determines the social categories that will have the greatest propensity to anomie, Durkheim's term for a state of deregulation.

The intrusion of social disorganisation was not Durkheim's explanation for the presence of crime. Rather, crime became pathological when, in response to disorganisation, it moved to levels beyond that which was "normal" for a particular society. The relevance of his approach to the situation we are trying to understand is therefore potentially considerable.

In applying Durkheim's ideas, later theorists have explained the impact of social change on rates of deviance through shifts in the criteria by which people assess their situation. What appear to be "objective" conditions take on a potential to engender stress in a manner that is understandable only in terms of how individuals perceive their situation. Proponents of the social disorganisation perspective, therefore re-framed the argument into one of relative deprivation, "the deprivation that arises not so much from the absolute amount of frustration as from the experienced discrepancy between one's lot and that of other persons or groups that serve as standards of reference" (Coser, 1970, p. 59).

The most ambitious attempt at formally linking social structure and crime within the social disorganisation rubric is Merton's (1957) anomie theory. For Merton, crime is one of several alternative responses to anomie, which he defines as a state in which culturally mandated goals fail to be relevant to the institutionalised means available for achieving them.

> Poverty as such and consequent limitation of opportunity are not enough to produce a conspicuously high rate of criminal behaviour. Even the notorious "poverty in the midst of plenty" will not necessarily lead to this result. But where poverty and associated disadvantages in competing for the culture values approved for *all* members of the society are linked with a cultural emphasis on pecuniary success as a dominant goal, high rates of criminal behaviour are the normal outcome (Merton, 1957, p. 147).

A criminal, therefore, is someone who retains the cultural goal of financial success, but finding himself or herself at a disadvantage in utilising the approved means for achieving it, substitutes a set of practices that are defined as unlawful.

When stated with such precision, the social disorganisation approach has not been sustained. The influence of anomie theory within criminology has dwindled, though Clinard and Abbott (1973, pp. 176–177) argue that some of its former lustre might be restored if it were deployed to explain recent trends in Third World nations. However, as a weaker assertion that change induces stress that in turn is manifested in crime, social disorganisation theories still form the bulwark of mainstream criminology: "As a country develops economically, and as this development is reflected in growing urbanization, crime generally increases rapidly" (Clinard, 1978, p. 1). The key appears to be the particular pattern of urban growth that emerges in response to industrialisation. In the general process of urbanisation, increased crime rates are identified with the upheaveal that occurs as a substantial proportion of the population shifts from rural to urban areas through migration and with the creation of slums, that persist, within those urban areas. These effects are compounded in the course of modernisation as people attempt to adjust to the new values and new institutions that are encouraged in cities.

There is sufficient coherence in recent theoretical and empirical work within the tradition to derive a set of basic tenets applicable to the Irish context. In so doing, particular attention has been placed on the work of Clinard (1942, 1964, and 1978), Clinard and Abbott (1973), Jacobson (1975), Webb

(1972), and Krohn (1978); these represent, to me, the most sophisticated modern exemplars of the social disorganisation tradition.

    (1) In a modernising society, sustained and rapid increases in crime rates emerge initially in urban areas. The resulting disparity in the incidence of urban and rural crime has been accorded the status of universal law by such writers as Clinard (1942) and Vold (1958, p. 188).

    (2) While crime directed at acquiring property is more prevalent in urban than in rural areas, offences against persons tend to be either evenly distributed or more prevalent in rural areas (Vold, 1941; Clinard, 1942; Henry and Short, 1954, pp. 90–94). Clinard (1942, p. 204) is the standard reference: "the influence of functional changes in a society is reflected far less in personal crimes than in property offences which involve the acquisition of things and not necessarily any personal or fortuitous situation". Property crime is associated with structural change; but murder, assault and other "person" crimes are assumed to be randomly distributed among the population or are considered as the product of a distinctive regional or subcultural normative system that encourages and facilitates interpersonal violence.

Therefore:

    (a) Urban-rural differences for property offences will exceed or be in the opposite direction to those for assaultive crimes.

    (b) The response of types of crime to structural change will show a clear sequence in which alterations in the pattern of property offences will precede those for person offences.

As specified by Jacobson (1975) for regional differences, this lag results when industrialisation and urbanisation generate socio-economic and demographic changes capable of shaping property crime patterns; the normative orientations that govern person crime rates, however, alter more slowly and therefore the implications for behaviour take longer to emerge. Of four recent tests of Durkheim's anomie theory using crime data, three (Jacobson, 1975; McDonald, 1976; Krohn, 1978) found marked differences between person and property offences in their relationship to socio-economic conditions; such differences, however, were not evident in Webb's (1972) study.

Other criminologists within the social disorganisation tradition, while agreeing that assaultive crimes tend to be more prevalent in rural than in urban areas, offer explanations that introduce considerations of structural differences between urban and rural areas. Henry and Short (1954; pp. 90–97), for example, argue that the greater strength of the "relational system" (primary group ties) in rural areas acts to direct aggression externally in the form of assaultive crimes that in urban areas would be directed internally and result in attempts at suicide. More generally, a social structure engenders pressures in the form of stress and coping resources that are unevenly distributed among the extant demographic and class groupings (Henry and Short, 1954; Bohannan, 1960; Wood, 1961). However, the most influential view is that of Clinard (1942; 1964), which precludes a link between structural change and assaultive offences.

A third expectation can also be identified: (3) Ultimately a stage is reached in which structural change extends beyond its urban base and permeates a social structure. As this occurs, a convergence in magnitudes and characteristics of crime ought to follow, erasing urban-rural and regional differences.

Finally, given the diverse and often vague usages of the term "social disorganisation," it is important to state my own understanding of what the term means. Social disorganisation refers to the absence of clear and agreed rules – a breach in the constitutive order of human activity. As such, it is not applicable to those situations in which one form of social organisation has successfully supplanted another, nor is it synonomous with situations in which there is a substantial level of deviant activity. Social disorganisation can be thought of independently of rule breaking behaviour (Cohen, 1959).

The Structural Perspective The societal changes that are the focus of writers within the structural perspective are as specific and commonplace as those of the social disorganisation perspective are general and abstract. The manner in which a society is organised, it is argued, shapes the major forms of individual and collective action available, including those that are regarded as criminal. Considerable attention is placed on the abundance and the distribution of property and on the availability of safeguards against the appropriation of property from its owners.

There are two recent instances in which this approach has been deployed as an explanation for long-term changes in crime statistics, a focus that makes them of considerable relevance to this paper. One study is part of an explicit challenge by Charles Tilly and his associates to the claims made by social disorganisation and relative deprivation explanations of collective violence and protest (Snyder and Tilly, 1972, Lodhi and Tilly, 1973; Shorter and Tilly, 1974; Snyder, 1975; Snyder, 1976; Snyder, 1978). However, in Lodhi and Tilly's (1973) study of nineteenth century France the purview is expanded to include patterns of crime. The trends in property and person crimes in France between 1831 and 1931 were used to compare the explanatory importance of the rate of urbanisation (representing disorganisation) to that of the structure of the urban setting itself. In Lodhi and Tilly's (1973, p. 313), view, "the geographic distributions of crime and collective violence do not correspond to the pattern of urban growth, ... urban settings, not the process of urbanisation as such, are conducive to crimes against property." Moreover, in the period during which urbanisation was proceeding most rapidly, the national crime trends show a decrease in the rate of property crime. Crimes against persons were essentially unrelated to any discernible pattern. In common with social disorgansiation theorists, Lodhi and Tilly (1973, p. 314) conclude that assaultive offences are independent of structural influences; variation in such offences is attributed instead to the "rules and expectations small groups learn in regulating their differences."

Three main variables emerged from the French data as explanations of variation in property crime rates:

> (1) the relative ease with which individuals can remove property from the control of other individuals and groups in one setting or another (which will, to be sure, depend on the definitions of "property" prevailing in the setting); (2) the ways in which different groups of poor people are drawn into the social organization of the setting, especially with respect to the general relations established between them and those in the same setting who control more property; (3) the extent to which acquiring property makes it possible for people to carry on their valued day-to-day activities and to which not having property makes these activities impossible. (Lodhi and Tilly, 1973, p. 315).

Essentially, this is an explanation based on opportunity, with the motivation to commit a crime being important only in terms of the legitimacy that is attached to property ownership. The focus is on the amount and the availability of property.

A second convincing and highly relevant application of the structural perspective is found in Cohen and Felson's (1979) study of recent American crime trends. In their formulation, a social structure establishes a particular patterning of "routine activities", and the distribution and level of crime follows the dictates of that pattern. It follows that a change in social structure will be linked to predictable changes in criminal activity. The logic of the link is summarised thus (Cohen and Felson, 1979, p. 589).

> We argue that structural changes in routine activity patterns can influence crime rates by affecting the convergence in space and time of the three minimal elements of direct-contact predatory violations: (1) motivated offenders, (2) suitable targets, and (3) the absence of capable guardians against a violation. We further argue that the lack of any one of these elements is sufficient to prevent the successful completion of a direct-contact predatory crime, and that the convergence in time and space of suitable targets and the absence of capable guardians may even lead to large increases in

crime rates without necessarily requiring any increase in the structural conditions that motivate individuals to engage in crime. That is, if the proportion of motivated offenders or even suitable targets were to remain stable in a community, changes in routine activities could nonetheless alter the likelihood of their convergence in space and time, thereby creating more opportunities for crimes to occur. Control therefore becomes critical. If controls through routine activities were to decrease, illegal predatory activities could then be likely to increase.

Explanation in such a perspective on crime trends is sought exclusively in terms of changes in circumstances; the questions of why particular individuals or which individuals will respond to those circumstances are not considered. Nevertheless, the perspective can account to an impressive degree for recent changes in both the level and pattern of crime in the United States.

The notion that the organisation of crime in a particular society (Gould, 1971), or in sub-areas of cities (Boggs, 1965) is a reflection of the social organisation of the setting has also been made using the analogy to a market place. In this view, variation in the prevalence of types of crime are to be understood as responses to a set of market mechanisms that are interconnected with those of the larger economy: "crime rates (at least for property crime) are not affected by individual criminality, but by variation in the supply of stealable goods, as well as the demand for goods to be stolen" (Mansfield *et al.*, 1974). The market place for crime, so defined, is governed by long-term changes in the abundance of property, which determines the profitability of crime as an economic activity. The focus is on the mechanisms which establish the supply of property available to be stolen at a level of risk acceptable to the participants in the marketplace – amateur and professional juvenile and adult criminals – and on mechanisms which establish the demand for stolen goods.

What unites the various studies cited, and justifies their treatment as a distinct perspective, is their focus on how changes in patterns of human activity and in the distribution of property together shape the level and pattern of crime. It is not change in itself that causes an increase in criminal activity, but a new structure of opportunities. Indeed, the opportunity for crime – or at least for property crime – is thoroughly rooted in the opportunity structure for legitimate pursuits and activities (see particularly Cohen and Felson, 1979). Therefore, the presence of crime, even substantial amounts of it, need not be indicative of disorganisation; it is instead a reflection of a more complex and more satisfying form of social organisation.

Generally speaking, those writing within the structural perspective are concerned only with crimes against property. An exception to this is Lane's

(1979) study of violent death in nineteenth century Philadelphia, which argues that industrial urbanisation had a beneficent impact on the level of crimes against persons. This occurred as the discipline acquired in the industrial workplace and in the public school system expanded to all contexts of urban life. The very changes in human activity effected by industrial employment inhibited violence by curbing the situations and opportunities in which it might occur. Life became more predictable, more controlled. The result was a diminishing rate of homicide.

While this fits unambiguously within the structural perspective, it remains at a very high level of generality. It does, however, seem possible to derive a set of expectations based on the nature of structural change for assaultive crimes such as homicide. That will be attempted in Chapter 6, which considers data on Irish homicide patterns.

The Implications of Change: What is Important?   Social disorganisation and structural perspectives on crime perhaps differ more in the explanations that they offer than in their implications. Both attribute to cities certain characteristics that lead to a departure from previous types and levels of criminal activity. Therefore, both draw attention to differences in the pattern of urbanisation in a society, one to the speed and timing of urban growth *per se*, the other to the speed and timing of particular changes in the urban context (such as the availability of property that can be readily stolen).

Where the perspectives differ most clearly is perhaps in what they were devised to explain. Social disorganisation tends to be most relevant for the level of crime, while changes in opportunities are likely to be most clearly reflected in the pattern of criminal activity. Since this study is interested in both topics, it is unnecessary, at least at this stage, to make a choice between the two perspectives. The main advantage of the structural perspective is that the societal changes that it emphasises can generally be expressed as variables. Those given prominence in the social disorganisation approach are less readily translated into specific variables; indeed, the level of crime is often appropriated as a measure of social disorganisation, a dubious procedure that in the present study would tend to lead to an obvious impasse.

Before examining some of the major features of Irish social change, two points which emerged from the discussion of the perspectives need to be elaborated. In both perspectives, the possibilities for variation in the depth and the pace of social change as well as its sequencing can be seen, but little guidance is provided on how that can be expressed. Also, there is an indication that the safeguarding of property from crime is at least partly dependent on the extent to which people accept the legitimacy of the distribution of property, but this argument is not developed.

Gerth and Mills (1953, p. 379) propose a continuum of change, "ranging from the relatively constant (for nothing is 'absolutely' static) through gradualist drift, deliberately piecemeal and cumulative reform, through a variety of breaks, discontinuities, and leaps, to total crises and revolutions". A useful theory will distinguish carefully between change accomplished by accretion and that arising from disjuncture. The institutions that dominated the social structure prior to the sequence of change at issue can be determined, as can the realignment among institutional orders fostered by that change. Secondary adjustments in the distribution of class boundaries, power, and status can also be traced. These questions are pertinent whether crime is attributed to the unsettling effects of change or tied to the nature of the emergent social order.

The diversity of social change and its consequences for crime trends has been most fully considered in the work of Clinard, and particularly in his studies of crime in developing countries (1973) and in Switzerland (1978). In contrasting the experience of those countries with that of the "typical" European and American model, Clinard cites the rate of urban growth (itself dependent on the nature of industrialisation) as manifested in the migration by rural youths to cities and the establishment of slums. In Switzerland, a gradual and restrained process of urbanisation ensured stability in the society generally and the absence of a substantial barrier between urban and rural areas. A low level of crime is the result. This contrasts with the rapidity and magnitude of urbanisation in the Third World, with consequent dislocations, heterogeneity, and slums – and a rapidly rising crime rate.

As the case of Switzerland suggests, there is sufficient diversity among Western "developed" nations to require a more detailed consideration of types of advanced capitalist society and the various paths taken in reaching that status. There is general agreement that the nature of urbanisation, as well as the other phenomena mentioned in summarising the two perspectives, are offshoots of industrial development. Now large-scale industrial expansion, wherever it occurs, inevitably re-orders the social structure, but it lacks a specific internal momentum. "In each country it takes place in specific social and economic conditions and is subject to direct and indirect national and international pressures" (Marceau, 1977, p. 4). When the focus is narrowed to industrial capitalism, the diversity of pathways to an advanced society remains considerable.

Comparative analyses by Moore (1966), Giddens (1973, pp. 139–155), and Marceau (1977, pp. 14–17), suggest two variables that combine to determine the path taken by particular societies. First, the class structure providing the framework for the decisive period of industrial expansion shapes the consequences that accrue: in England, the framework was a developed and stable bourgeois order; in Germany, industrial growth preceded the emergence of such an order and was undertaken instead through the initiative of a state controlled by the traditional land-owning elite. Second, societies differ in the duration and intensity of the period of decisive industrialisation. England is the archetype of gradual and early industrial growth, and France of a protracted and uneven industrialisation that culminated in a post-Second World War spurt of massive and rapid industrial expansion. Generally, the more recently manufacturing became the predominant force in an economy, the more swiftly that transformation was accomplished. It will be necessary to locate Ireland among these alternatives.

A second issue that needs attention is the role played by the nature of property. Since the bulk of the criminal law is devoted to activities that involve the acquisition of property outside of the legally and morally sanctioned market and inheritance arrangements, it is necessary to understand the meaning and the legitimation of property within a social structure. It is not merely the amount, distribution, and character of property that potentially change but the extent of consensus on the validity of the concept of property itself. Property, whether physical or otherwise, represents a specification recognised in law and culture of certain rights constraining others to behave in a particular manner toward an object.

If the level of acceptance afforded the definition of property on which the criminal law is based changes over time, then an increase in the rate of property crime seems likely. There is some evidence to suggest that such a change is one concomitant of the general impact of industrialisation and urbanisation. In urban settings, it becomes increasingly difficult to perceive a particular item of property as belonging to a specific individual; the association specified in the law becomes more abstract. Though such a change cannot be expressed as a variable, it is of considerable importance in understanding the high rate of property crime that seems characteristic of the advanced societies. Portable forms of property – cars, television sets, radios, phonographs, and records – all become more available. At the same time, a more instrumentalist view of the rights to such property is likely to develop. This need not be associated with the more basic issue of the acceptance of the right to privately owned capital. The most valuable property in any urban setting is, of course, land and the legitimacy of private ownership of property in that sense can be unquestioned at the same time that other forms of property, which are mass produced and lack any distinctive connection to the owner or to his livelihood, become increasingly seen as valid targets for acquisition without benefit of purchase.

In criminological theories, the meaning of property is generally considered in the context of the extent of integration of young people into the larger society. The possibility that "subcultures" or "contracultures" will develop, formed primarily of young males rejecting the norms obtaining generally within a society, is stressed. Clinard (1978) in his study of Switzerland attaches considerable importance to the high level of conformity by Swiss youth and the level of communication between adults and youths. Since in most countries property crime is primarily accounted for by young people, Clinard explains Switzerland's low rate of such crime as largely a reflection of the degree to which a distinctive youth culture, which opposes basic rules of adult behaviour, has not developed.

The Irish Context

This section attempts to sketch the broad outlines of social change in Ireland during the post-Second World War period. The two perspectives summarised in the preceding section were the main guides in selecting topics for discussion. First, the general nature of industrial growth in Ireland will be considered, followed by the pattern of urbanisation that this fostered. Other aspects of Ireland's social structure will be treated that seem sufficiently distinctive to shape trends in the level and pattern of crime.

The Pattern of Industrial Development   With the impetus of *The First Programme for Economic Expansion*, which was launched in 1958, Ireland entered an unprecedented period of rapid and sustained industrial development. By 1961, the effect was clearly identifiable in the main economic trends in the form of an acceleration in growth (Kennedy and Dowling, 1975, pp. 3–8). Between 1951 and 1971, industrial growth and a decline in agricultural employment forged a substantial change in the Irish economy. From a male work force that in 1951 was nearly one-half engaged in agriculture (46.7 per cent), and roughly one-quarter in each of industry and services, the 1971 profile had shifted to 30 per cent in agriculture, 32 per cent in industry and 31 per cent in services (Hannan *et al.*, 1980). (Those "out of work" form the remainder of the labour force.) The expansion in the scale of industrial enterprises was also marked: in 1948 the average manufacturing enterprise had 38 employees; the comparable average for 1968 was 60.

Two disjunctures in particular combined to mark a break with preceding trends in the relationship between societal characteristics and crime in Ireland. The first disjuncture originated in the agricultural sector. During the 1940s Irish agriculture, which had been static in structure and output for more than half a century (Crotty, 1966, p. 84), began to be transformed by mechanisation and commercialisation. This marked the final stage in the destruction of the tradition and insular rural world so distinctly described by Arensberg and Kimball (1940). The processes of accommodation and adaptation to new economic and social realities during the 1950s were later intensified and redirected by a second disjuncture effected by the unprecedented industrial growth of the 1960s. The 1960s, therefore, represent both the culmination of the response of the breakdown of the traditional system and the aftermath of sudden industrialisation. The 1950s and the 1960s, therefore, can be singled out as periods of secondary social change during which institutions and roles adjusted to major disjunctures in social structure.

There was considerable dislocation in both periods. For the 1950s, the mass movements of population through emigration and internal migration appear to suffice as justifications for putting forward the expectations of social disorganisation theory. However, it is likely that the depth of social structural change needed to support the arguments of structural theorists was not present until the mid-1960s, when the clear commitment to fostering capitalist industrial development as the mainspring to prosperity began to be reflected in the occupational structure. Therefore, the sequencing of sustained movements in the crime statistics, like urban/rural differences, can potentially serve as guides to the plausibility of the alternative theoretical perspectives. It must be stressed that the sequencing of trends and the urban/rural differences found in the crime statistics can facilitate interpretation but cannot definitively choose the more powerful approach.

Ireland represents a clear instance of late and sudden industrialisation. But unlike France, where a stable and well-differentiated class system was in existence to engineer the final movement to an advanced capitalist society, there was an essentially pre-industrial class structure at the point of critical growth. The one group with the necessary entrepreneurial tradition and skills for constituting an industrialising elite – the old Protestant business families – was too intimately tied to the discredited colonial elite (Fogarty, 1973, p. 115). Where industrial growth was evident, state sponsored enterprises were the vehicles. In consequence, the post-1958 period of sustained economic development forged a new class structure. In France, the redistributions accompanying the comparable post-War growth amounted to minor variations on the extant class structure. Irish industrialisation, however, altered the composition of classes and the degree of class structuration creating hitherto non-existent boundaries. Change occurred not by accretion but by disjunctures in the total social structure.

That the pattern of industrial development was diffuse rather than concentrated in a few major urban centres also had important consequences. The attraction of the cities as targets for migration was thereby lessened, as was the level of internal migration generally. Also, the sequencing of secondary adjustments to structural change was probably less clear and important than it was in most European countries. The impact of social change was more evenly felt throughout the society, and the filtering process by which change begins in major urban centres and only gradually spreads to other areas less pronounced. This does not mean that every region and type of area shared equivalently in the changes, but that rapidity and lack of concentration lessened the differences that emerged.

Urbanisation and Emigration   The impact of this pattern of industrial development on urban growth is not difficult to document. Dublin, in contrast to most capital cities, was not the magnet for a massive wave of rural migration, and the growth of Dublin was gradual and largely from natural increase.

Certain aspects of Irish emigration patterns, and particularly their impact on urbanisation, also cast doubt on the applicability of social disorganisation theories to Ireland. Of the characteristics of emigration in this century, one of the most distinctive is that it was a movement of individuals more than of families. Emigrants typically were young, unattached, and, at least before the 1950s, drawn from those without marketable skills (Meenan, 1970). Massive emigration meant that Ireland became an urban nation by default – that is, through rural depopulation rather than by the characteristic European process of migration from rural areas into the towns and cities (Walsh, 1974). Therefore, Dublin and other Irish cities did not share with other European cities the catchment role of sheltering and socialising successive waves of rural migrants. Evidence from the Dublin Social Mobility Study indicates how striking a departure this was from the European pattern: non-Dublin born Dublin residents were on average of higher social status and educational attainment than native Dubliners (Hutchinson, 1969).

The relationship between internal migration and emigration to other countries is certainly distinctive to Ireland. In the 1946–61 period, only eight of every 100 migrants from outside of the capital had Dublin as their destination; this had increased for 1961–71 to 21 out of every 100 (Hughes and Walsh, 1980, p. 54). It was only in the latter period, in which the level of emigration declined markedly, that Dublin acted as a significant magnet for the rest of the country, and particularly for the young and well educated. In both periods, however, the Dublin born were considerably less likely to emigrate than were those born elsewhere. Taken together, the post-1961 attraction of Dublin for migrants, the high rate of natural increase in the Dublin population, and the low emigration rate of Dubliners contributed to the growth in the city's population.

The growth of Dublin can be charted from the data in Table 1. While the increase between 1926 and 1971 in both the size of Dublin's population and in the proportion of the national population living in the city was substantial, it was spread fairly evenly over the period. In the years after 1961 the pace quickens, for reasons noted above, but the trend of increase was spread over a period of decades rather than concentrated over a short interval. Emigration

Table 1: *National, County Dublin, and Dublin urban area populations at each census from 1926 to 1971**

Census Year	National	County Dublin	Dublin Urban Area[1]
1926	2,971,992	505,654 (17.0%)	439,205 (14.8%)
1936	2,968,420	586,925 (19.8)	507,888 (17.1)
1946	2,955,107	636,193 (21.5)	550,725 (18.6)
1951	2,960,593	693,022 (23.4)	634,473 (21.4)
1956	2,989,264	705,781 (24.4)	649,338 (22.4)
1961	2,818,341	718,332 (25.5)	663,389 (23.5)
1966	2,884,002	795,047 (27.6)	734,967 (25.5)
1971	2,978,248	852,219 (28.6)	778,127 (26.1)

*Numbers in parentheses are percentages of national population.
[1]The Dublin Urban Area in this table consists of Dublin County Borough and Dun Laoghaire Borough with, from 1951, the Suburbs adjacent to them. The definitions of Borough and Suburb are those used in each year's Census, with one exception; to take account of the creation of Dun Laoghaire Borough in 1930, as well as a major extension of the Dublin County Borough, the figures for 1926 are based on the definitions of 1936.

was one factor underlying that pattern of urban growth. Though this changed after 1961, the level of Irish internal migration, including that with Dublin as its destination, remained low by European standards (Hughes and Walsh, 1980).

The 1960s and 1970s were periods of substantial dislocation for the Dublin working class. Dublin Corporation's housing policies created massive movements of families from traditional working class neighbourhoods to new housing estates and blocks of flats away from the city centre. Taken together, urban growth declining emigration, and working class dislocation did in the 1960s – probably for the first time since the foundation of the State – approximate the image of social change that underlies the social disorganisation perspective.

Another important consequence of emigration can be seen in the changing age structure of the population. The proportion of the total accounted for by those age groups most prone to involvement in crime was depleted: the size of the group between ages 15 and 29 declined by 11.6 per cent between 1926 and 1971. Even during the last five years of that period, during which the numbers in that age category increased, without emigration the increase would have been 10 per cent higher (Central Statistics Office, 1973, pp. xvi–xvii). Differences in the age structure of urban and rural areas are also noteworthy: in

1971 24.8 per cent of the Dublin population was within the 15–29 age category; outside of Dublin the corresponding figure was 20.9 per cent.

During the 1950s, the distinctive Irish pattern of rural to urban migration blunted the impact on cities of rural change. Emigration overseas absorbed the bulk of those dislocated in the course of farm mechanisation. When migration to the capital became important in the 1960s, those migrating were drawn primarily from the rural, well-educated middle class. In this way, the consequences of the marginalisation of a substantial proportion of the labour force was deferred at least for a time by the safety valve of emigration. Between 1951 and 1971, 543,000 persons – a number equal to nearly one half of the total labour force at the latter date (Walsh, 1974, p. 107) – emigrated. Dublin was spared the role of absorbing massive numbers of rural migrants.

Emigration possibly supplemented its general role as a safety valve reducing pressure from the young with limited opportunities with a more specialised form of emigration:

> An Irishman with criminal aspirations almost invariably leaves this country and goes to England, sometimes voluntarily, sometimes on the advice of the police or even a District Justice (Russell, 1964, p. 146).

This specialised emigration may be tied to many of the same factors Walsh (1968) identified for emigration generally, chiefly short-term fluctuations in the supply of employment in Ireland and in England. In sum, the impact of emigration in the 1950s, and probably earlier, was to limit rather than to enhance the potential for deviance.

The Meaning of Property Property in the form of farm land traditionally carried decisive weight in shaping the magnitude and nature of crime in Ireland. During the nineteenth century, until the right of land tenure was ultimately secured in the 1880s through the Land War, agrarian unrest was reflected in high levels of "crime" in British government statistics (Broeker, 1970, p. 239). Perhaps in conjunction with the advent of mass education, the achievement of widespread land ownership appears to have effected a transformation to rates of violent crime that approach the inconsequential. Subsequently, agrarian unrest would recur, but only at brief and mild interludes. A decrease in the traditional estrangement between the population and the imposed legal order is also identifiable, though later events were to, at least temporarily, recreate the breach. In Lynch's interpretation (1966, p. 52), the 1880s marked Ireland's social revolution. Land ownership facilitated the development of a peasant system, with a deep, emotional, attachment to property. The symbolic importance of land was embedded in the conservatism of the rural social order. Given the proportion of the population with rural backgrounds, it is probable that the symbolic meaning of property associated with subsistence and semi-commercial farming areas persisted in the larger society until supplanted in the course of industrialisation.

Property rights, therefore, existed in a context conducive to a high level of legitimation. Legitimacy refers to a state in which compliance with a set of rules derives not from force of habit or from an assessment of the benefits of so doing but from "a conviction of the moral dutifulness of obedience" (Poggi, 1977, p. 321). Property still had a meaning in terms of a person's livelihood. With increasing access to mass media from other countries and declining agricultural employment, such treatment of property could not be sustained.

This coincided in the 1960s with a transformation in the range and amount of consumer goods available in Ireland, both urban and rural. The change in the availability of property is perhaps most clearly shown through the growth between 1951 and 1975 in the number of privately owned motor vehicles. In 1951 there were 96,714 licensed vehicles, a figure which by 1962 had increased to 207,166, by 1968 to 336,615, and by 1975 to 511,827. The 1951–1975 increase is more than five-fold. In *per capita* terms, the increase was from 3.3 per 100 in 1951 to 16.4 per 100 population in 1975. Information on the number of television sets in the Republic are only meaningful for the period since 1962, the year in which RTE started television broadcasting. There were 93,000 licensed television sets in 1962, 377,000 by 1968, and 564,880 by 1975. This translates into an increase from 3.3 to 18.1 per 100 population. The 1962 to 1975 change in number of sets is six-fold comparable to an increase for those years of 2.5 fold in the number of private motor vehicles. (Statistical Abstract of Ireland, various issues and McCarthy and Ryan, 1976).

The Legitimation of British Law in Ireland   The retention of English criminal law by the newly independent Ireland negates a basic assumption of the social disorganisation perspective.[1] To Durkheim, a society's legal code is the "visible symbol" of its social solidarity: "We can thus be certain of finding reflected in law all the essential varieties of social solidarity" (Durkheim, 1933, pp. 64–65). The criminal law inherited from England, developed in the

---

[1]The retention of the institutional arrangements characteristic of nineteenth century British industrial capitalism as the framework for the traditional, rural, and Catholic Irish Free State is an unresolved problem for Irish historians and sociologists (Lynch, 1966; Williams, 1966). It also highlights ambiguities in the Weberian approach to the legitimation of social structures: if legitimation is accomplished by intrinsically moral principles that instil a sense that obedience has a value, as Weber's followers argue (cf. Blau, 1964, pp. 200; 254–255; Parsons, 1949, pp. 670–677), how was it possible for the "value consensus" in Ireland during the 1920s and 1930s to legitimate the institutions inherited from British rule?

nineteenth century to contain disorder in the industrial cities of the most advanced of the capitalist societies, would seem to have little affinity to the consensus constructed around Catholic values and principles that most observers
regard as the dominant force in independent Ireland. Such a gap makes less
plausible the social disorganisation argument that rapid increases in the level
of crime occur in response to a weakening of attachments to societal norms.
That attachment seems tenuous from the start.

The criminal law involves more than a set of rules and procedures for its enforcement; a particular concept of crime and of criminals is inherent to it.
Both the rules and the concept of crime they imply bore little obvious
relevance to Ireland prior to the 1960s. However, as Ireland changed in the
general direction of advanced capitalism, the inherited legal system became
more relevant. To me, this seems to reverse the basic argument that is made
in most social disorganisation approaches: rules are being institutionalised
instead of being erased.

Conclusion: The Applicability of Perspectives on Crime

The process of social change in Ireland, at least as I have described it, does
not conform to the main assumptions of the social disorganisation perspective. Like Switzerland (see Clinard, 1978), Ireland appears to be a distinct
case; unlike Switzerland, however, the distinctiveness does not necessarily
imply a low and invariant crime rate. What is most distinctive about Ireland
since the 1950s is the nature of urbanisation, which seems to me to preclude
an application of the major tenets of social disorganisation explanations of
crime trends. If such explanations are applied to Ireland, however, then it
seems plausible to anticipate upward trends in the crime rates commencing in
the 1950s not in the 1960s.

What deserves emphasis in recent Irish experience is the suddenness,
rapidity, and pervasiveness of change. Industrialisation, which is the primary
force, explicitly or implicitly, in most attempts to explain the growth of crime,
occurred later and more quickly than in other countries. The gradual accommodation to change stressed by Clinard in his study of Switzerland is hardly
applicable to Ireland.

In terms of the likely timing of a change from fairly constant levels of crime
to rapid and sustained increases, it seems reasonable to focus on the early
1960s. If an increased crime rate is one of the secondary adjustments that follow in the wake of concentrated industrial development, then certainly by the
mid-1960s the impact should be identifiable. Also, the rapidity and extent of
the structural changes ought to be reflected in a more diffuse distribution of
increasing levels of crime than was found in other countries. The sequencing
of increases in crime, with an initial impact on the largest urban centres that

only gradually spreads to smaller cities and, after a considerable lag, to rural areas, is unlikely.

The changes experienced in the 1960s are not irrelevant to the arguments contained in the social disorganisation perspective. Rather, the timing and the distribution of rising crime levels is likely to be different from that found in other countries. Undoubtedly, the very complexity of life that emerged in the aftermath of economic change acted to loosen, for many individuals, constraints that previously had acted as effective means of social control. Social disorganisation was a factor in what occurred, but it was not as decisive an influence as has been claimed for most western and developing nations; it certainly is less easy to pinpoint.

What a social disorganisation perspective cannot hope to explain is the change in the pattern of criminal activity. In particular, the possibility that crime not only becomes more prevalent but more sophisticated is not readily considered within that framework. However, it is the possibility that crime is not only becoming more frequent but also more sinister, in terms of the damage inflicted on life and property, that makes crime a topic of public concern. The structural perspective is more amenable to answering issues related to that concern. Changing opportunities, in the form of the portable goods available to be stolen and the efficacy of the protection afforded such property, necessarily exert considerable influence on the pattern of crime that will obtain. The perception of the relevant forms of property is also likely to change in a manner that reduces inhibitions toward theft.

The use of a structural perspective seems preferable in the Irish case for a more basic reason. If change is sudden and diffuse, the plausibility of a social disorganisation explanation for long-term changes in the level of crime seems quite limited. If an entire society becomes sufficiently disorganised to engender substantial changes in the level of crime, then the continuation of routine human activities becomes questionable. In the absence of a specific location for the disorganising impact of change – such as large urban areas that absorb the main force – the applicability of the entire approach becomes tenuous. A structural perspective, in which changing social organisation has certain implications for the level and pattern of crime, appears to be more useful if the changes of interest lack a specific locus.

For these reasons, the arguments put forward by proponents of the structural perspective appear to be more convincing guides in interpreting the crime trends that later chapters will describe and analyse. When the momentum of economic change accumulated to a significant degree, re-ordering the structure of work, family, and leisure, the activities that are defined by the criminal law as punishable offences also experienced a transformation comparable in depth and permanency. This is not to deny that the changes

Ireland experienced were often disruptive, requiring adjustments that posed significant problems for many individuals. But I believe that the emphasis in explaining what has happened should be placed on the distinctive social changes of the past three decades. What may at times have seemed to be a growing disorder can, I think, with hindsight be shown to have been the establishment of a new order.

Chapter 3

Data Sources: Availability and Adequacy

The perspectives outlined in Chapter 2 seek to explain trends in the level and pattern of criminal activity. Crime statistics, however, as they change over time, reflect many things, of which actions that violate the criminal law statutes are but one. Public concern over crime and confidence in the police, as well as the manner in which the police are organised and in which they collect and classify their information all potentially vary from year to year, thus changing the crime statistics. This chapter undertakes the groundwork necessary to use the Irish crime statistics between 1951 and 1975 as indicators of changes that occurred in crime. It considers the sources of published information and evaluates their relevance to the issues outlined in Chapter 2. This leads to the selection of a set of meaningful indicators of changes in crime from the published data and from supplementary information collected specifically for this study. It is then possible to examine methods that can be used to describe the relationship between the selected indicators and social change.

Sources of Data on Irish Crime

Information on crime and law enforcement in Ireland is primarily to be found in two documents. Since 1947, a *Report on Crime* has been published annually by the Commissioner of the Garda Siochana. This report provides a breakdown of the incidence, detection rate, and judicial disposal of cases for approximately 125 specific offence categories. The report also details the age and the sex of those persons convicted for each category of offence and provides information on special garda programmes such as the Juvenile Liaison Officer scheme. For certain broad summary classifications, the numbers of known and detected offences are stated for individual garda divisions and districts, and, where relevant, information is provided on the resulting monetary losses during the twelve months. The second basic document is the *Annual Report on Prisons and Detention Centres,* in which, for each year since 1928, the numbers and the characteristics of those committed to the prison system are tabulated.

Other relevant statistics can be found in the section on Reformatories and Industrial Schools (from 1970–71 onwards referred to as Special Schools and Residential Homes) in the *Annual Report of the Department of Education.* Also, for each financial year, detailed information is available on government expenditures relevant to law enforcement and to the courts. These are included as separate sections for the Office of the Minister for Justice, for the Garda

Siochana, for the prisons, and for the courts in the *Appropriation Accounts*. For all of these annual reports, the *Statistical Abstract* includes a summary of the most important statistics. In the period preceding the publication of the annual *Report on Crime*, the *Abstract* was the only source for crime statistics.

Irish crime statistics, like Irish criminal law, can best be described as a British legacy. The basic format of the *Report on Crime* is an improved version of nineteenth century reports on crime in England and Wales. This similarity is a reflection of the extent to which compilation of crime statistics in Ireland has been, and is, an annual ritual, with publication of the report the sole objective. With the exception of occasional references in Dáil debates, crime statistics are rarely used. This does not preclude some use of the crime statistics within the Garda Siochana in reaching decisions on manpower allocations. Also, the Conroy Commission in its report (*Commission on the Garda Siochana*, 1970, p. 46) did make some use of offences-known figures and (1970, p. 26) reviews the work of the Urwick, Orr and Partners consultancy report of 1957 in which criteria for allocating the force's manpower to rural areas were partly based on the number of indictable offences reported. There have been two recent attempts of analysing crime trends in Ireland. Hillyard (1969) examined trends in crime and law enforcement over the 1901 to 1967 period, with particular attention to 1955–1967. Bacon and O'Donoghue (1975) carried out an economic analysis of crime covering the years 1952 to 1971.

The lack of a clear purpose to which crime statistics are applied has three basic consequences. First, the format of the report is now anachronistic and in need of revision. Second, inconsistencies and ambiguities have not always been challenged and improvements have not been suggested. Third, with ease of preparation a major criterion for selecting what is to be included, a gradual reduction in the range and depth of the information contained in the report has taken place.

Still, what is available for Ireland is impressive when compared to the deficiencies found in crime statistics elsewhere. A continuous series can be assembled of offences known to the gardai that commences in 1927. Moreover, the statistics reflect a data collection process that, in contrast to those in the United States and England, is undertaken at a national level, employing a consistent set of definitions and rules for classifying and counting offences. Crime statistics in Ireland are essentially compiled at the level of the 100 garda districts. In contrast, the US Federal Bureau of Investigation merely collates the returns submitted to it by thousands of state, county, and municipal police departments; its control over the classification and counting processes that underlie the statistics published is minimal. These virtues of the Irish crime statistics are greatly enhanced by the detail of reporting. From 1927 to 1946 the annual *Statistical Abstract* used some 40 reporting categories, while the introduction of a report exclusively devoted to crime statistics in 1947 expanded the coverage to 75 categories, a number that has since increased. The flexibility this gives to users of the data is invaluable, as is the potential for ensuring comparability among offence categories over the years even if some categories become aggregated.

The merits of Irish crime statistics are offset, at least in part, by certain disadvantages. Many of these arise from sheer disuse: ambiguities are present in the reporting practices simply because no system of annotation accompanies the statistics, to publicise and update the definitions and procedures being used. While even the incessantly used, some would say overused, American crime statistics are apparently routinely misinterpreted (see Steffensmeier, 1978, pp. 580–581), there are formidable difficulties involved in treating the Irish crime statistics as a time-series. The remainder of this section details hazards specific to the Irish Crime Statistics, while the section that follows evaluates those statistics in the light of problems inherent to all attempts at measuring crime through police records.

News media coverage of the Garda Commissioner's annual report tends to be dominated by a single statistic: the total for all indictable offences. Whatever its merits as a legal distinction, the contrast between indictable and non-indictable offences fails to isolate a reasonable index of the level of crime: indictable offences range from murder to shoplifting. The emphasis given to the total of indictable offences, and the four traditional subdivisions thereof, limits the usefulness of much of the information published. Also, such conveniently packaged measures are irresistible temptations to those seeking a simple answer to a very complex problem, that of determining how much crime is present.

Since some reliance on the indictable/non-indictable distinction is unavoidable, it is useful to make clear its basis. Indictable offences are those that can, or must be, tried before a jury, as defined primarily by statutes in 1849 and 1851 (Bartholomew, 1971, pp. 1–12). The "can or must" leads in practice to a diminution of any clear difference based on seriousness. Today, many, perhaps most trials for indictable offences are held summarily before the District Court, without a jury. In 1972, 91.6 per cent of all commitments to prison were from summary proceedings in the District Court. The set of categories that by the criteria of mid-nineteenth century legal thinking were "serious", does not, for us, represent a cohesive or particularly important indication of the level of crime. Even the four subdivisions for indictable offences – offences against the person, offences against property with violence, offences against property without violence, and "other" offences – subsume so diverse a set of offences as to be meaningless.

Another legacy of the nineteenth century is the reversion in the 1958 *Report on Crime* to the use of a crime year in which the time period covered is the twelve months commencing on the 1st October. This practice, which was used in England during the 1850s (Tobias, 1972, p. 298), contrasts with the 1947–1957 and post-1974 practice of using the calendar year. As a time-series in their own right, the crime statistics are rendered awkward by the shift in the reporting period. The last three months of 1957 are included in both the 1957 and 1958 *Report on Crime,* and the last three months in 1974 are not included as part of an annual tabulation, though the figures for those months are appended separately to the 1974 report. Awkwardness can turn into confusion if the crime data for the 1960s and 1970s are used in conjunction with annual statistics on economic conditions. A study testing the hypothesis that crime increases in periods of high unemployment will, unless corrections are made, involve an assumption that unemployment in 1971 has some impact on offences that occurred in 1970, since the 1971 *Report on Crime* includes data from three months of the previous year. The introduction of a "lag", which argues that economic conditions require an interval before exerting their effect, removes that anomaly but introduces its own disparities. In the 1960s and the first half of the 1970s, the interval will be three months shorter than for other periods.

Other changes accompanied the 1958 alteration of the reporting year. The amount of information provided on the processing of juveniles through the law enforcement system was curtailed and the dividing line between major and minor larceny was changed from £5 to £50.

There is further ambiguity in the selection of counting units. The unit for indictable crimes is the offence, but one offence can reflect the actions of any number of individuals, and one person can be responsible for, or charged with, any number of separate offences. It is, therefore, impossible, given the absence of an enumeration of persons, to discover what proportion of those charged with a criminal offence were convicted, sentenced to prison, tried before the District Court, discharged, or otherwise treated. Further, since only one entry is possible for each offence, where the result is mixed, with some defendants being guilty and others not guilty, the entire offence is entered as leading to a conviction. In such information as is provided for individuals on the number, age, and sex of those convicted – a person is only entered for the most serious offence. In the 1974 report, non-indictable offences, previously tabulated on the basis of individuals, are made comparable to the reporting procedures for indictable offences. As a result, the pre-1974 figures on non-indictable offences cannot be reconciled with more recent information.

Another difficulty is that each report refers only to events within the 12 months covered. While all the offences listed as "known" will have taken

place, or have been detected, within that 12-month period, the court actions
and the characteristics of those convicted can, in the 1947 to 1975 reports,
relate to offences that took place in previous years. It is, therefore, impossible
to determine precisely the detections and court proceedings resulting from a
given year's offences. Furthermore, as the number of known offences has been
increasing from year to year, the lag between offences and detections can
result in a spuriously low detection rate.

A final limitation of the present *Report on Crime* is the absence of data per-
taining to individual counties or cities. As a result, comparisons between
types of areas cannot be made and socio-economic factors in the distribution
of crime cannot be analysed. The number of known and detected offences in
the four traditional aggregate categories of indictable offences is provided for
each of the 18 Garda Divisions and for the Garda Districts of four major
cities, but the boundaries of those jurisdictions are generally incompatible
with other administrative units and the categories used are comprised of offences so diverse as to render the figures meaningless.

Evaluating Crime Statistics

An assessment of the meaningfulness of crime statistics can only be made
on the basis of the purpose for which they are to be used. As Hindess (1973)
argues, "different theoretical problematics must produce different and
sometimes contradictory evaluations of any given set of statistics." The
relevance of the conceptual categories used in generating the statistics, and
that of the rules and procedures employed in assigning individual cases to
those categories, takes precedence in the evaluation. For example, Hobsbawm and Rudé (1969, pp. 54–60) convincingly use poaching as an index of
rural economic conditions and social tensions; it is unlikely that the offence of
embezzlement would in such a context prove as useful.[2]

For the present study, the primary requirement is that the indicators
selected be reasonable measures for the rate of change in the level and the pattern of criminal activity. This is essential if changes in the crime statistics are
to be considered as responses to social change. The crime statistics, therefore,

---

[2]An exemplary use of crime statistics toward a clear theoretical purpose can be found in
George C. Lewis's 1836 survey of agrarian disorder in Ireland. He divided serious offences
recorded during 1833 into two classes: those intended to create a general effect of deterring or
compelling others, and those in which the intent was limited to a specific purpose, such as acquiring money. Lewis (1977, p. 78) observes: "Now the characteristic difference between the
crimes of Ireland, and of England, France, and indeed of almost every civilized country in the
world, is that in a large part of Ireland the former class appears to preponderate considerably
beyond the latter: whereas, in other countries, the former class of crimes is so small that at ordinary times it can scarcely be said to have any existence."

must be an accurate measure of changes that have taken place in Ireland over the past quarter century in both the magnitude and the nature of criminal activity. In terms of magnitude, it is essential that trends reflect the pace of change. But the indicators must also allow for the possibility that trends in the level of offences will be accompanied by changes in the characteristics of criminal acts, particularly in the degree of sophistication and organisation involved and in the seriousness of the resulting damage. The offence categories should be sensitive indices of the possibilities for substantial appropriation of property through law-breaking activities. Indicators of person offences that, by definition, do not involve an attempt to appropriate property can then be used for comparative purposes.

Within this broad specification of requirements, it is possible to begin considering the technical criteria that underlie the choice of crime indicators. The use of police and judical statistics to quantify the extent of crime has a history of nearly two centuries, and the controversy over the merits of that practice is equally venerable. From the early nineteenth century, the debate that centred on the possibility that the under-reporting of criminal offences to the police, together with the selective recording of those cases by the police, creates a "dark figure" of crime not included in the official statistics.[3] This raises two issues: first, the possibility that the published figures seriously under-represent the occurrence of major crime, and second, the possibility that the process by which offences become "known" is so random that comparisons of crime rates between years are invalid.

The first issue may not be quite as serious as it seems. Chapman (1970, p. 82) argues, that "the complexity of administration in modern societies is such that if all laws and police ordinances were to be universally enforced, all citizens would be criminal." As was noted in Chapter 1, it is necessary to be more precise in defining what is of interest. This will clarify the magnitude of the problem involved in the "dark figure" by attributing to it degrees of importance that vary between types of offence. The level of under-reporting is high only for relatively minor offences, such as petty larceny (Ferdinand, 1967; Hindelang, 1974); the reporting of offences such as homicide and robbery appears to be quite representative (Archer and Gartner, 1976; Vigderhous, 1978; Messner, 1978, p. 5). The problem posed by limitations in

[3]In particular, great attention was given to statutory changes and changing court practices as alternative explanations for observed changes in the crime statistics. Thus, Durkheim in *Suicide* (1951, p. 338) comments: "No doubt, property crimes have decreased since 1854 while suicides are increasing. But this decrease is in part fictitious; it is due merely to the fact that at about that time judges began to send certain crimes before the courts of summary jurisdiction"; for Karl Marx's observation on this same "artificial" decrease, see Taylor, *et al.* (1973, pp. 216–217). Tobias (1972) devotes a chapter to a description and evaluation of the crime statistics of that era.

the range of offences that are reflected in the official statistics also varies greatly by country. Strong evidence suggests that under-reporting is far less prevalent in most countries than in the United States (Verkko, 1953; President's Commission of Law Enforcement and the Administration of Criminal Justice, 1967, p. 20; Clinard, 1978, pp. 57–60).

Thus for many categories of crime, and perhaps for the most important categories, the "dark figure" is less menacing than is sometimes thought. A series of British studies has recently considerably increased our understanding of the process through which offences become "known". Bottomley and Coleman (1976), for example, examined police files in a medium-sized north of England city and found that only 13 per cent of known indictable offences were discovered by police, the remaining offences coming to light either through the initiative of the victims or of other members of the public. In the absence of evidence that witnesses or victims are unduly reluctant to report offences through fear, or through a conviction that police inefficiency makes it pointless to do so, it may be concluded that much of the "dark figure" consists of acts considered trivial or private by most people. To the extent that the public is indeed the major arbiter of what becomes known and therefore included in the crime statistics, a basis exists for considering offences known to the police as a relatively sensitive measure of crime. A substantial research literature attests to the primary role of offence seriousness in determining whether an incident is reported to the police (see especially Skogan, 1976 and Hindelang, 1976).

The second technical issue is the possibility that systematic changes over time in the propensity of the public to report crimes, or in the police practices in processing those reports, invalidate comparisons between years in the number of known offences. Quetelet, the nineteenth century Belgian statistician who produced the seminal work on crime statistics, adopted an assumption that the amount of "known" crime bears a constant relationship to the amount of crime that remains unrecorded. The validity of that assumption is likely to vary among types of offence and among countries in accordance with the seriousness of under-reporting, as noted above. As Cohen and Felson (1979, p. 588) observe, an upward trend in the crime statistics reflects both an increasing number of offences *and* an overall increase in offence seriousness.

The difficulties in establishing the representativeness of police crime data are exacerbated by a necessary reliance on criminal law categories. Enactment of new statutes can render the revised classification system irreconcilable with that which previously obtained. Even if stability in legal definitions can be assumed, there is an inherent ambiguity in the failure of statutory offences to be mutually exclusive – a marked increase in, say, indictable assaults might merely reflect a change in the convention by which a police force distinguishes between indictable and non-indictable assaults. An important principle for making such distinctions in the criminal law is intention; as a criterion for classifying behaviours into offence categories, this poses obvious difficulties. Motivation, however, is not generally used in defining statutes, and this precludes consideration of differences among incidents in that regard, say, that between robberies with a political and those with a non-political motivation.

New statutes often appear to be attempts at removing ambiguities in existing criminal law. For example, the *1961 Road Traffic Act* created a new offence, "taking a motor powered vehicle without authorisation," to deal with instances in which no clear intention to permanently deprive the owner of his or her property was present. Under the provisions of the Larceny Act of 1916 such intention was required, and where it was absent recourse had to be taken to a charge of larceny of the petrol consumed in the journey, for which intention could be established. In this instance, the impact on the validity of trends in motor vehicle larceny was minor, but in other cases a new statute might artificially change the level of pre-existing categories.

To the extent that uniform classification and counting procedures are followed by a police force, the possibility of bias being introduced into comparisons of annual crime data is reduced. In England and Wales, it was not until after the Second World War that a systematic recording procedure for offence and arrest data was established and distributed to all police authorities (Downes, 1965). Inconsistencies remained, however, and in the mid-1960s the Perks Committee reviewed the data collection process underlying the criminal statistics. Three basic problems were identified (Departmental Committee on Criminal Statistics, 1967, p. 18):

(a) Some types of offence consist of more or less continuous, or repetitive, activity, which cannot without some arbitrary convention be counted as a definite number of distinct occurrences.

(b) Several different people may be the victims of the same criminal act.

(c) Some criminal acts involve the infringement of a number of distinct parts of the criminal law, but an element of unreality would be introduced into the statistics if each infringement were counted as a separate offence.

The solution adopted for these problems, or the failure to mandate a solution, will have a considerable impact on the apparent magnitude of the crime problem in a police jurisdiction. For example, if the number of larcenies in one country is established on the basis of victims, counting each series of offences directed at an individual or an institution as one offence, it is pointless to compare that figure with that from another country that counts each appropriation of property as a separate offence. One final complication deserves mention: the classifying and counting conventions employed for offences that are "detected" can differ from those for which no suspect is found (Departmental Committee on Crime Statistics, 1967, p. 18). If a suspect has been identified, the choice of offence categories will be made in terms of strategy for future court proceedings. The general tendency is to specify more but less serious offences when suspects are available than when they are not.

In Ireland, clear rules for classifying and counting are set down in the Garda Siochana Code. For purposes of interpreting the number of known offences, and for comparison with other countries, the two most important rules are:

1   A larceny, fraud or forgery directed in a continuous series against one person or institution will count as a single offence.
2   A forcible entry into a block of offices or flats will be counted according to the number of separate offices or flats entered. If, however, one flat or office is entered and property taken from several individuals, there was only one forcible entry but as many larcenies as there were individuals who lost property.

The implementation of these rules on a national basis substantially increases the confidence that can be placed in the Irish crime statistics. However, it remains useful to bear in mind the possible deficiences of all such statistics when used in time-series analysis. The following check-list is a guideline for interpreting trends in known and detected offences:

1   Changes in statutes
2   Changes in public attitudes
   (a) tolerance of particular types of crime
   (b) approval of and confidence in the police
   (c) ease of reporting offences to the police
   (d) inducements to report offences – insurance or other forms of compensation for injury or loss that require a police report
3   Changes within the police
   (a) classification rules
   (b) counting rules
   (c) resources (size of the force and its budget)
   (d) method of patrolling
   (e) detection rate
   (f) tolerance of particular types of crime
   (g) activities of "private" police – security firms, etc.
   (h) changes in police chief or commissioner

In summary, the under-reporting of crime is of great or little moment in establishing the validity of official crime statistics depending first, on one's purpose, second, on the types of offences involved, and third, on the location of the study. By focusing on the major offence categories most implicated in the transformation of property and other structural relationships, it appears possible to minimise the problems inherent in official statistics.

Alternative Data Sources

Dissatisfaction with police crime statistics in recent years prompted the development of two alternative data collection techniques by criminologists – victimisation and self-report surveys. Both have been used extensively to complement or supplant official crime data. Victimisation studies employ the approach of public opinion sample surveys, requesting a randomly selected group of households or individuals to list all incidents in which they felt themselves to be victims of a crime, regardless of whether the incident was reported to the police. Such surveys pose serious problems of designing samples and of constructing items that respondents can meaningfully answer: where the questions are phrased so that people can understand and therefore give reliable answers, the responses often cannot be reconciled with the legal definition of the offence (Hood and Sparks, 1970, pp. 25–32; Gibbs and Erickson, 1975; OECD, 1976).[4]

Self-report studies use surveys of selected groups – typically school children – to find the assessment individuals make of how often they have committed a crime. Establishing the comparability of the resulting answers to the official crime data is also a problem here, though reservation about the accuracy of the responses given, both in terms of exaggeration and concealment, is the main reason for scepticism (see Hood and Sparks, 1970, pp. 66–70 for a detailed discussion). Certainly the use of polygraphs to verify the "confessions" made in self-report studies was inconclusive (Clark and Tifft, 1966). It is also necessary to consider the likely restriction of such surveys to schoolchildren: who else can be induced to co-operate in such a venture? But the most compelling arguments for caution are perhaps ethical, not methodological.

While the above assessment is perhaps too severe – after all, both techniques are more representative than police crime statistics – the successful application of either victimisation or self-report studies is limited to appropriate research questions. Hirschi's (1972) use of a self-report survey to assess theories of delinquency causation and Clinard's use of victimisation surveys

[4]Victimisation surveys, which were initiated and popularised in the United States, present difficulties if applied in other contexts. Where a phenomenon whose incidence we wish to estimate is very sparsely distributed over a national population – and property crime victimisation in Ireland, even if seriously understated in police statistics, is infrequent – the standard errors will be such as to make the results unilluminating. Essentially such a survey can confirm that victimisation is low, but the estimates will be too imprecise and unreliable to be of use as a series of annual statistics.

to study crime in Switzerland are examples. However, for the present study, in which the central question is the nature of changes over the past few decades, neither technique can be very revealing; the official crime statistics are the only relevant data. A continuous series of annual data is required that goes back at least to the mid-1960s.[5]

Crime Indicators

Three main options exist for obtaining a more precise basis for assessing the trend in reported crime than that forthcoming from the total number of indictable offences. An index comparable to the US Federal Bureau of Investigation's Crime Index can be prepared, summing the incidence of a few selected serious offences.[6] Such indices, along with a deceptive air of precision, have the disadvantage of accurately describing trends only in periods when the component offences are either all increasing or all decreasing at a uniform rate; where some offences are changing more rapidly than others, an index obscures far more than it reveals (Blumstein, 1974).[7] A second, more flexible, approach is to establish categories, where the criterion is the homogeneity of the behaviour involved in the offences rather than any legal distinctions. Where even such categories appear to be too broad in what they include, a third option is to remain faithful to a single statutory definition of an offence.

The approach adopted here is a combination of the second and the third option. For property offences, the selected offence categories are burglary (subdivided into housebreaking and shopbreaking),[8] larceny of motor vehi-

[5]Other sources of data on property crime trends include theft and burglary insurance claims and premiums (Clinard, 1978) and consumer expenditure on burglar alarms and other security equipment. Attempts to compile such data for Ireland proved unsuccessful.

[6]The FBI crime index is computed as the unweighted sum of seven "index crimes": criminal homicide, forcible rape, aggravated assault, robbery, burglary, auto-theft, and larceny over $50. The first four offences constitute the index of "personal crime", with the remaining three representing the property offence rate.

[7]"The point is applicable to any set of indicators composed of heterogeneous components. When the set of phenomena comprising the index move together, then virtually all indexes are equally useful, since the results are insensitive to the particular form of the index. On the other hand, when there is internal diversity in the movement of the components comprising the index and unless there is some 'natural' commensuration measure (like price, with which the economists are blessed), then the internal variation among the components will be reflected one way in some indexes and in another way in other indexes" (Blumstein, 1974, p. 864).

[8]That distinction was eliminated by the Criminal Law (Jurisdiction) Act, 1976 which also created a new offence of aggravated burglary (in which a real or imitation firearm or explosives are used). The *1977 Report on Crime* reflects that change.

cles, larceny from unattended motor vehicles, receiving stolen property, and robbery. These will be complemented by the use of indictable assaults as an indicator of offences against persons. The value of property stolen in burglaries will be used as an index of the seriousness of that offence. The *Report on Crime* gives a figure that represents an estimated value for all property stolen through burglary in that year. This yields two measures of the changes that occur in "seriousness" for that offence category. The total estimate can serve as an indication of the magnitude of the financial loss sustained. A second indicator can be derived when the total loss is divided by the number of burglaries in which property was stolen. What results is the *average* financial loss, a figure which can rise or decline independently of the total value – if the total value increases but the number of burglaries expands by a greater proportion, the net result is a declining average loss from burglaries.

The nine main indicators and the comparable reporting categories as given in the 1972 *Report on Crime* are:

1. Assault ("wounding and other acts endangering life, felonies", "assault, wounding and other like offences, misdemeanours").
2. Housebreaking ("burglary"; "housebreaking, dwelling houses").
3. Shopbreaking ("breaking into shops, warehouses, etc.")
4. Larceny from vehicles ("larceny from unattended vehicles")
5. Robbery ("robbery with arms"; "robbery and assaults with intent to rob"; "demand or robbery of arms").
6. Receiving ("receiving stolen goods").
7. Larceny of vehicles ("larceny of motor cars"; "larceny of motor cycles, scooters, etc."; "larceny of motor lorries"; "larceny of other mechanically propelled vehicles").
8. Pedal cycle larceny ("larceny of pedal cycles").
9. Average property value (the total value of property stolen through "offences against property with violence" divided by the number of cases in which property was stolen).

These specific indicators were selected to represent the diversity of property offences, and some contrasting offences against persons, while retaining the most reasonable claims to representativeness and to providing levels for which differences between years reflect actual changes in prevalence. It is to be stressed that the most important feature of the indicators is that the trends reflect changes in levels and patterns of crime, not that the levels shown are precise enumerations of all instances in which a particular law is broken.

For all of the offences except homicide, the most serious threat to such an assumption is the possibility that increases in police resources, both in manpower and in equipment, between 1951 and 1975 contributed to the observed trends in the crime indicators. That possibility will be considered in Chapters 4 and 5, in which the trends are described and interpreted.

Two main time-series were compiled from the annual totals of known and detected offences in the chosen categories. The first series is derived from the national level data contained in the *Reports on Crime* covering the years 1951 to 1975. Complementary data on economic and social conditions and on law enforcement resources and activities are available.

Through unpublished data abstracted from garda records, it proved possible to disaggregate the national totals into areas, making possible urban and rural trends for the 1964 to 1975 period. Comparisons can be made of the level and trend of recorded crime in three types of areas: the Dublin Metropolitan Area; the next four largest urban centres – Cork, Limerick, Waterford, and Galway – combined; and the remainder of the country, which is labelled non-urban. Boundary changes in 1963 made earlier disaggregations impossible.

The three "areas" used are based on the reporting units for which information could be obtained. Garda Districts, while constructed out of District Electoral Divisions, do not coincide with those of other basic administrative units. Broadly speaking, the boundaries of each of the five urban areas selected for particular attention encompass the city proper, the contiguous built up areas of dense population, and a substantial part of the rural hinterland oriented towards the city. The Dublin Metropolitan Area, so defined, included an estimated 990,160 persons in 1977, representing 31.3 per cent of the national population. The other four cities together housed an estimated 353,700 persons in that year, equivalent to 11.2 per cent of the total population. The 1,818,200 individuals included in the residual category of non-urban areas are therefore diversely situated. The residents of 11 towns which in the 1971 Census were each over 10,000 in population fall within that area-type, as do residents of isolated farm houses. Despite the heterogeneity of the non-urban category, the three-fold division of areas approximates the important urban/rural differences.

In presenting offence levels, the convention of computing *per capita* crime rates is generally ignored. For the national trends between 1951 and 1975, the population variation is too slight to make a noticeable difference in the trends. In the case of the disaggregated data, the necessary population base is unavailable for the denominator. Virtue, however, partly overshadows necessity. Gibbs and Erickson (1976) and others have expressed serious misgivings on the use of *per capita* crime rates. Unless a jurisdiction constitutes a self-contained, "ecological", community, its population understates the pool of potential victims and offenders. The ease of movement and communication across most internal boundaries largely invalidates the size of the local population as an important explanatory factor in the study of crime.

The published statistics on homicide were supplemented specifically for this study by obtaining full descriptions of all homicides recorded in the years 1951 to 1960 and 1970 to 1974. In this way, it will be possible in Chapter 6 to examine the actual events that for all other offence categories are reduced to a single increment in the annual total. Information was compiled from the Garda Siochana files on the characteristics of the victims and the offenders, on the location of the offence, and on the relationship between victim and offender. With that information, a far more ambitious analysis of changes in homicide patterns can be undertaken than for the other offence categories.

In analysing these time-series the primary objectives are to discern the nature of the trend underlying the recent increase in Irish crime rates and to determine the extent to which that trend is responding to social change or to cyclical factors such as the unemployment rate. Social disorganisation and structural approaches make claims as to the nature of crime trends and the relationship between crime rates and other socio-economic variables that to some degree conflict.

Statistically, crime trends tend to assume one of three major forms. One is that of a constant growth trend throughout the post-Second World War period, with the crime rate increasing by an absolute amount or a percentage rate of change that is invariant. Growth can also be achieved by a curvilinear trend in which the rate of increase rises in the course of the series. A third possibility is that no one trend can be isolated – an abrupt and irreversable shift in the trend itself and/or in the relationship between the trend and other forces occurs at some point in the course of the series. Such a transformation (in the statisticans' terminology a "structural change", a phrase this paper has already overburdened with nuances of meaning), requires that a series of trends or relationships be identified. The discontinuity is too great for one trend line or one set of parameters to be considered.

In the Irish situation over the quarter century being examined, a trend of growth, either constant or curvilinear, seems most appropriate to the arguments contained within the social disorganisation perspective. The alternative of a structural change, a statistical watershed in the series, corresponds to the basic assumptions of the structural perspective. That one type of trend can be identified as characteristic of the period does not, of course, confirm that the perspective with which I have identified it is the most useful. Rather, the contrast between types of trend will hopefully be useful in making sense of the crime trends that will be found in Chapters 4 and 5.

Chapter 4

National Level Crime Trends: Description and Analysis

This chapter begins the attempt to characterise and to interpret the changes that have taken place in the level and pattern of crime in Ireland over the last quarter century. Using the nine indicators described in the preceding chapter, national level trends in the level and pattern of criminal activity are described and then analysed. The first task is to determine the magnitude of the change in the indicators: to what extent has crime become more prevalent and more serious over recent years? In terms of explaining what occurred and of predicting what is likely to happen in the 1980s, however, the amount of change is of perhaps secondary importance to the nature of the trends. Several possible specifications of upward trends in the crime statistics have already been given. The main contrast will be between increases accomplished by accretion and those that occur through a clear structural break in the series. In addition, the sequencing of sustained and rapid annual increments in the statistics can be compared for various types of offences. Both the overall assessment of the nature of the increases registered and the comparison of types of offences can then be examined in the light of the two perspectives on crime trends discussed in Chapter 2.

The examination of national crime trends unfolds in the following order. In the section that follows, the overall trends for the nine indicators will be examined, first graphically and then statistically through regression and correlation analysis. An assessment can be made at that point as to the magnitude and nature of the increases that in fact occurred over the 1951 to 1975 period. In a separate section, the relationship between trends for property crime and the availability of property will be considered, a relationship of direct relevance to the structural perspective on crime. The relationship between economic conditions and crime will then be examined for all nine indicators, reflecting the possibility that either the trend itself, or the departures from trend of levels in those indicators is a response to economic forces. Such a relationship is one hypothesis that has been derived from the social disorganisation perspective (e.g., Pierce, 1967). As a result of the data analysis, it will be possible in a concluding section to make an assessment of both the dimension and the meaning of the changes in the crime statistics that have become so important a public issue.

The Growth of Crime: 1951–1975

The examination of the nine national level indicators begins with consideration of the trends created by changes in levels of incidence over the 25 years at issue. This will provide a rough measure of the magnitude of the change we are trying to understand and a description of the manner in which it has come about. The focus will be on the contrast between two periods: 1951–1963 and 1964–1975. The pace of change in each period will be assessed, as will be the sequencing of sustained series of annual increases or decreases. This will first be done by charts, with the visual appraisal augmented by index numbers that summarise the amount of increase for three periods: the 13 years prior to 1964, the 12 years in the post-1964 period, and the full 25 year time span. The graphic presentations will be followed by a statistical comparison of 1951–1963 trends with the trends prevailing in the 1964–1975 period.

There are nine indicators. Eight separate offence categories were selected on the basis of their meaningfulness as time-series indicators and as representatives of the major types of property that are targets for criminal activity: housebreaking, shopbreaking, larceny of motor vehicles, larceny from unattended motor vehicles, pedal cycle larceny, receiving stolen property, robbery, and indictable assault. In addition, the value of property stolen each year through burglary (housebreaking and shopbreaking combined) will be used as an indicator of the seriousness of that form of property crime.

Graphic Presentation of Crime Trends   Figure 1 charts the changes in the levels of housebreaking and shopbreaking offences recorded by the Garda Siochana between 1951 and 1975. The post-1964 increase for both offence categories is striking, particularly when contrasted with the cyclical fluctuation in the pre-1964 pattern. When the increases are translated into index numbers, the comparison between periods is more precise, though the increase is so pronounced as to render the numbers almost superfluous. When 1951 is set at 100.0, the level of offences for housebreaking in 1963 is 134.3 and for shopbreaking 154.5; if post-1964 offence levels are standardised to the first year of that series, the housebreaking index in 1975 is 426.7 and that for shopbreaking is 316.6. The break that occurs in the mid-1960s emerges unambiguously in the figure: it is decisive and permanent. Until about 1964, there was only slight upward movement in either series. While there is some suggestion in Figure 1 that the trend over the full 25 years is curvilinear, time-series analysis that will be presented in a later section reinforces the stronger indications of the presence of two distinct trends.

That the watershed for both offences occurred in the mid-1960s strengthens the argument that associates the immediate aftermath of industrial development and economic expansion with a powerful effect on Irish crime patterns. Similarly, the possibility that a fundamental transformation occurred at that point in the link between socio-economic conditions and crime is made more plausible by the consistency between the two indicators. But it cannot be denied that it is the magnitude of the upward trend that demands the most attention: over the 25 years a six-fold (an index number of 610.9) increase in

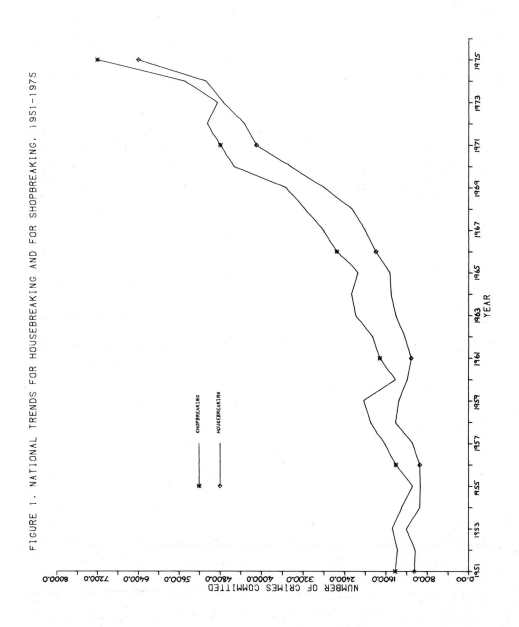

FIGURE 1. NATIONAL TRENDS FOR HOUSEBREAKING AND FOR SHOPBREAKING, 1951–1975

housebreakings and a five-fold increase (index number of 507.0) in shopbreakings are registered. For both shopbreaking and housebreaking, the increase is highly concentrated in the post-1964 period. Prior to that, there is no discernible pattern to the changes from year to year.

In all 25 years, the number of shopbreakings exceeds that of recorded housebreakings, with particularly marked differentials in the 1960s. However, given the more pronounced upward trend, after 1964, in burglaries which have houses as their targets, by the early 1970s the differential has narrowed. Still, the consistency over the 25 years is remarkable, especially given the fluctuations recorded for both offences in the 1950s.

The availability of annual data on the total value of property stolen through burglary allows a comparison of the increase in recorded levels of offences with an indicator of the seriousness of the damage sustained. Such a measure can also, but less directly, reflect the degree of organisation and sophistication that characterise burglaries. Figure 2 is, therefore, of particular interest. It shows for the 25 years the average value of property stolen, with the value deflated for all years into constant (1953) prices. What emerges is a somewhat blurred image of the trends found for recorded levels of offences. The lack of focus stems from the disordered fluctuation during the 1950s and from the absence of a clear break in the early 1960s. That a break occurs is evident in Figure 2. However, the seriousness of the loss accompanying the average burglary tended to decline during the 1950s, and while this ended when a sustained upward trend began around 1963, it is difficult to locate the precise point of the break. The upward trend, once commenced, continued, with a slight tapering off in the late 1960s, to 1975.

The contrast between the trend for the average value of property stolen in burglaries and the trends for housebreaking and shopbreaking incidence is perhaps best expressed in the index numbers. With 1951 set as 100.0, the level in 1963 is 74.1 and that in 1975 is 148.6. Even in the 1964–75 period, where a clear upward trend can be identified, the increase results in an index number of 181.9.

This contrasts sharply with the six-fold and five-fold increases registered for the offences through which the property was misappropriated. Therefore, while the financial loss inflicted through burglary has increased, particularly in the last dozen years, and while this can be interpreted as a consequence of a shift toward "professional" burglars, the rate of increased incidence has outspaced any changes in the nature of the offences. It is also possible that the change in the amount of property stolen merely reflects the greater availability of property in the more typical targets of the burglar. A later section will return to that possibility.

Figure 3 provides further evidence on the change in the degree of financial

FIGURE 2. AVERAGE VALUE OF PROPERTY STOLEN IN BURGLARIES (IN CONSTANT, 1953 PRICES), 1951-1975

loss experienced annually through burglaries. It charts the change in the total value of property stolen both in current prices and in constant prices (again expressed by deflating to 1953 prices.) However measured, the magnitude of the increase over the 25 years is dramatic, though it is naturally more formidable in the case of the undeflated figures. Both measures also evince an almost unvarying level throughout the 1950s and the early 1960s. In the mid-1960s, this changes through a sustained series of substantial annual increases, the largest of which occurs between 1969 and 1970. It was in those years that the incidence of both housebreaking and shopbreaking registered one of their sharpest increases. Evidence to be presented later will suggest that the turn of the decade was marked by very considerable changes in the operations or procedures of the Garda Siochana, and the increase in burglary offences will be returned to in that context.

The major finding in Figure 3 is that trends in the total value of stolen property reiterate those found for offence levels. The break in the mid-1960s is unmistakable, and the post-1964 increase substantial indeed. The index number for 1975 describing the increases since 1964 is 839.8, while that for 1963 expressing the change over the previous 13 years is 102.9. For the full 25 years, the final index number is 694.1. If "seriousness" is defined in terms of the total value of stolen property, then obviously burglary is substantially more serious a problem than was the case in the early 1950s or even the mid-1960s. However, given the increase in the number of burglaries that contribute to that total value, the change in the seriousness of the average burglary has not been particularly marked. In 1953 prices, the average loss sustained in a burglary was £33 in 1951, £27 in 1964, and £49 in 1975.[9]

[9]The stolen property for which the *Report on Crime* provides an estimated value, includes cash, luxury items such as jewellery, electric appliances, and ordinary household goods, including food and clothing. For cash, the most reasonable base by which to take inflation into account when comparing value over time is the Consumer Price Index (CPI). However, since the prices for certain goods of considerable interest to burglars, such as electric appliances, have risen less rapidly than the CPI, the average values shown in Figure 2 understate somewhat the increase in "seriousness". That possibility is best expressed by a comparison of the CPI with a price index based on household durable goods (electric and gas appliances, furniture, linen, etc.). Over the full 25 years, and for the two sub-periods of 1951–63 and 1964–75, the prices of household durables rose less rapidly than the CPI. For the most important period, 1964–75, the CPI rose by 3.09 and an index based on durable goods only by 2.68. Thus, the use of the CPI does understate the real increase that has taken place in the average value of stolen property, but only slightly, as a substantial proportion of the property involved should be deflated by the CPI. The effect of my choice of the CPI as the most appropriate basis for deflating the average values can be seen in the results of substituting a price index based only on household durable goods: the average values in constant (1953) prices in 1964 and 1975 would be £31.11 and £53.22. (The price indices are adapted from Central Bank of Ireland, 1977.)

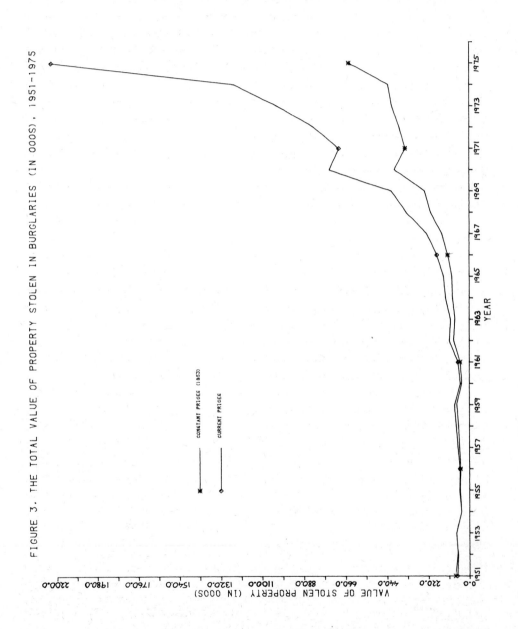

FIGURE 3. THE TOTAL VALUE OF PROPERTY STOLEN IN BURGLARIES (IN 000S), 1951–1975

Thus, though burglary may have become a more substantial problem, costing far more in real money terms with each passing year since the mid-1960s, it is not the case that burglaries have become more serious as criminal incidents. If changes had occurred in the nature of property crime, bringing to its accomplishment enhanced sophistication and organisation, then surely the average value of the loss would have risen substantially. It did not, and it therefore seems reasonable to conclude that though there is undoubtedly more crime today than before, the evidence suggests that it is more of the same; unlike many occupations, burglary apparently has emerged from the 1960s and 1970s relatively unchanged. This refers, of course, to the average burglary, a statistical artifact that given the large numbers involved may mask the presence of a few burglaries displaying a sophistication and gaining a profit hitherto unknown in Ireland.

Overall, for burglary, it can be concluded that the total value of stolen property increased at a rate during the 25 years that was slightly faster than for the number of recorded burglaries. The result is an average value that increases in the post-1964 period, but at a moderate pace.

The trends for the two offences involving motor vehicles – larceny of vehicles and larceny from vehicles – can be gauged by examining Figures 4 and 5 (while the offence indicators are grouped two to a figure, the grouping must be based on matching comparable ranges of levels). Neither pattern departs substantially from that revealed by the burglary indicators. Cyclical variation in larceny from vehicles before 1964 results in no real increase in the level recorded. That pattern is reversed in the years after 1964, with especially sharp increases registered in the late 1960s and early 1970s. For larceny of motor vehicles, a form of property not readily available in the 1950s (there were 43.7 private motor vehicles per 1,000 population in 1955 and 132.0 per 1,000 population in 1970), the trend in the first period differs from that for larceny from vehicles. Though the number of stolen motor vehicles is small throughout the 1950s, a trend toward increase is clear. However, like the offence of stealing from an unattended vehicle, the rise after the mid-1960s is very rapid indeed, particularly after 1967. In both indicators, a level of saturation appears to have been reached, at least temporarily, in 1972. This consistency is remarkable, for though both offences have motor vehicles as their target, the offences are not similar in what they involve, and they differ particularly in the value of the property stolen.

When the increases are expressed as index numbers, these observations are made more concrete. Between 1951 and 1963, the increases result in index numbers of 419.1 for larceny of vehicles and of 115.4 for larceny from vehicles. If the 1964 totals are set equal to 100, by 1975 the index number for the former offence is 744.7 and for the latter offence 490.9. Thus, for both

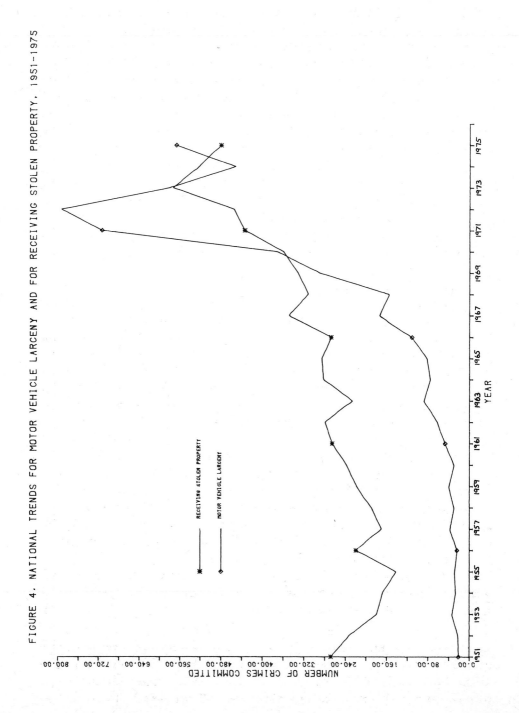

FIGURE 4. NATIONAL TRENDS FOR MOTOR VEHICLE LARCENY AND FOR RECEIVING STOLEN PROPERTY, 1951-1975

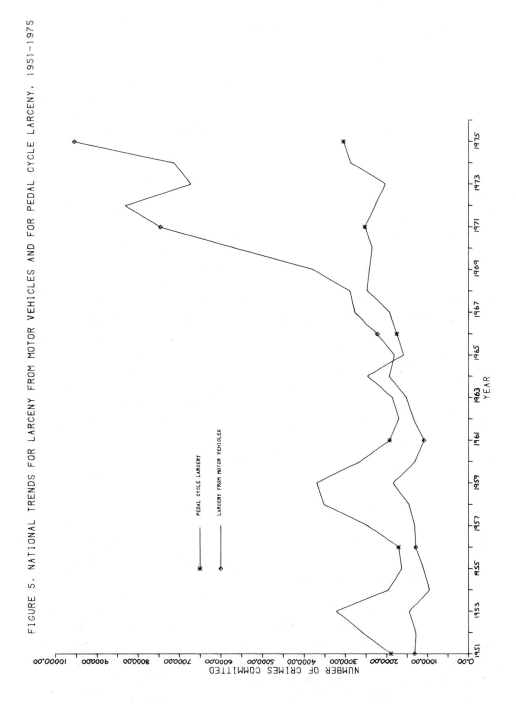

FIGURE 5. NATIONAL TRENDS FOR LARCENY FROM MOTOR VEHICLES AND FOR PEDAL CYCLE LARCENY, 1951–1975

indicators the increase after 1964 was considerably greater than that registered previously.

The levels both of burglaries and of larcenies involving vehicles are potentially responsive to changes in the distribution of property. Where an offence category specifies that a motor vehicle must be the target, however, it is likely that variation in levels recorded will be sensitive to a set of supply and demand factors that depart from those operative for other forms of property. Comparison of the five indicators examined thus far suggests this is indeed the case. Where a vehicle is involved, though the break in the data on burglary is replicated, the trends after 1964 are in many respects distinct, particularly in the magnitude of the early increases and the establishment of a plateau in the early 1970s. If the vehicle itself is the target, the distinctiveness is also identifiable in the early period: while other indicators fluctuate, larceny of vehicles experiences a four-fold increase.

Larceny of pedal cycles, the trend of which is shown in Figure 5, provides data on another specific form of property. Like motor vehicles, pedal cycles offer the convenience for those wishing to steal them of a valuable object combined with a form of transportation. Throughout the 25 years, the level of recorded larcenies of pedal cycles fluctuates quite systematically, at first rather expansively in five-year intervals and later in more controlled movements of shorter intervals. As a result, the level recorded in 1975 falls below that typically found in the 1950s. Indexing the changes by setting 1951 levels equal to 100.0, the 1963 level is found to be 98.6. When 1964 figures are used to gauge the change, the 1975 level stands at 123.1. In both periods the changes in pedal cycle larceny do not resemble those found for the other indicators of property crime. The offence appears to be governed by considerations different from those obtaining for major property crimes.

Returning to Figure 4, the trend in receiving stolen property offences can be examined. The main outlines of the pre-1964 fluctuation and the rapid increase thereafter are readily detected for this offence. By 1974, however, the recorded level had peaked, and the direction of the trend marked by the last two years of the series is that of decrease. The trend for receiving offences is of interest, first, because it conforms to what was identified for other property offences and, second, because of what it suggests about the changes taking place in the organsiation of property crime. Like the other indicator of the degree of organisation – the average value of stolen property – the trend for receiving is more modest than that for levels of property offences. The index numbers for the first period result in a 1963 index number of 84.7 and for the later period a 1975 index number of 169.3. Over the full 25 years, the level recorded has less than doubled. If it is true that a thriving market in stolen goods requires a network of middlemen, then the limited increase since 1964 in the number of such individuals arrested (as will be seen in Table 3 that offence is rarely recorded in the absence of a "detection") supports the impression that the nature of crime has not greatly changed.

This cannot be said for the offence of robbery. Figure 6 traces the long period of essential stability in that indicator up to 1964, that yields to increases, at first gradual, and then to a six-year sequence of rapid increases. Perhaps the nature of the change is best described in this way: there were 24 robberies recorded in 1951, 42 in 1963 and 704 in 1975. Translated into index numbers, the 1951 to 1963 increase can be stated as 175.0, and the 1964 to 1975 increase as 1,135.5. The precise point at which the break in the series occurred, however, is difficult to determine; certainly it lacks the clarity that characterises the trends for other property offences. Another feature of the trend is more recognisable: a tapering off in the early 1970s of the pattern of increase. In sum, robbery, like larceny of vehicles, seems to be governed by considerations that are in some respects distinct from those obtaining for less specialised forms of property crime.

The preceding eight indicators all described offences directed at acquiring property. Assault, the final indicator to be examined, is used to represent the incidence of offences directed against persons. Though levels of homicide and assault correlate at .87 for the 1951 to 1975 period, this can be attributed entirely to the strength of the relationship after 1964; the correlation between 1951 and 1963 is .01. Caution is therefore necessary in generalising the findings for trends in assault to the entire category of interpersonal violence, however, it does provide a useful contrast to the property crime indicators examined thus far.

Figure 6 indicates that the increases in indictable assaults have been consistent throughout the 25 years, the only exceptions being two brief stable periods, one in the early 1950s and the other in the mid-1960s. When expressed as an index number, the increase over the first 13 years of the series is 293.3. The increase after 1964 is slightly less: if the 1964 level is set to 100.0, the index for 1975 is 229.8. However, over the full 25 years, the level of assault increases seven-fold (indexed as 682.3). In 1951, a total of 164 indictable assaults were recorded nationally; by 1963 this had risen to 481 and by 1975 to 1,119. At least on the basis of the trend shown in Figure 6, it is not possible to assert that the break identified in all the other series took place for assault.

It is also clear from Figure 6 that the upward movement in assault levels preceded comparable periods of sustained increases in property crime. Even the level of motor vehicle larceny did not definitively depart from a cyclical pattern until the early 1960s, nearly ten years after that had occurred for assault. Therefore, the only offence that began its ascent in the 1950s is the one not directed at obtaining property. Assault is also the only indicator with a

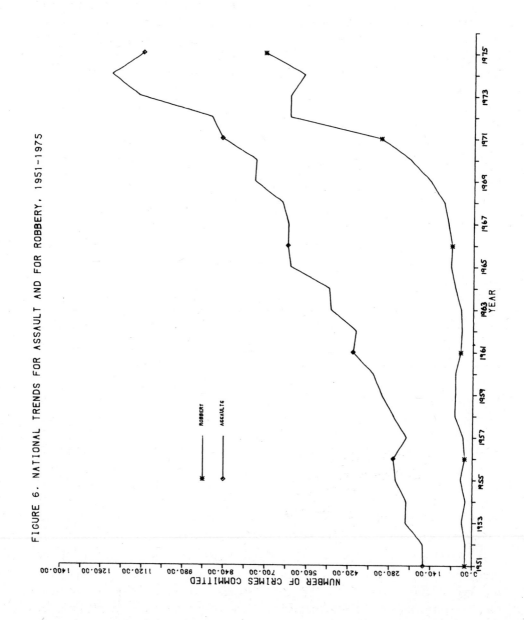

FIGURE 6. NATIONAL TRENDS FOR ASSAULT AND FOR ROBBERY, 1951-1975

trend for which a structural break is not clearly identifiable.

The change in the level of incidence for assault, though not the sequencing of periods of substantial increase, is similar to that found for homicide, the other indicator of crimes against persons. Homicide includes both murder, where there is a presumed intention to kill and manslaughter, in which death need not have been intended. There were, on average, 7.2 such offences in the 1951 to 1963 period (standard deviation of 3.4) and 16.4 in the post-1964 years (standard deviation of 5.4). This contrasts with average numbers of assault of 286.2 and 807 in the two periods, respectively (with standard deviations of 92 and 228.7). This consistency between two indicators enhances the confidence with which we can evaluate the increase that occurred in the level of violent crimes against persons. Of all offence categories, that of homicide is least subject to the problems of under-reporting or classification error. As will be seen in Chapter 6, while the published Irish data on homicide require extensive re-working to form a consistent series, the adjustments are feasible; for all other offence categories, such changes cannot even be attempted.

If the nine crime indicators on which I have focused are accurate guides to what has taken place between 1951 and 1975, then a substantial increase in the level of crime cannot be gainsaid. For most offences directed at acquiring property, the magnitude of that increase makes depressing reading: in 1975, there were six times as many housebreakings, five times as many burglaries, 27 times as many larcenies of motor vehicles, seven times as many larcenies from motor vehicles and 29 times as many robberies recorded as were recorded in 1951. Moreover, for all those offences, the bulk of the increase was crowded into a ten-year period. A watershed clearly did occur in the mid-1960s, marking what will, undoubtedly, prove to be a permanent departure from the previous low levels of crime. Crime has become a more acute social problem.

But what is most ominous is that crime occurs more frequently. There is no basis for asserting that an equally dramatic change occurred in the pattern of crime, as represented by its seriousness. Over the 25 years, the average value of stolen property in burglaries has only slightly increased, at least if inflation is taken into account. Though the increase in the number of robberies suggests that a change in the most common types of crime may be occurring, the evidence is inconclusive. Certainly, the relatively small increase registered in the level of receiving stolen property offences argues against the image of crime being pursued today in a manner that is far more sophisticated, more efficient, or more organised than hitherto.

Trends in Garda Resources and Operations The trends in the nine indicators examined through the preceding charts are all based on the offences that are "known" to the gardai *and* that were subsequently entered into the official statistics. It was argued in Chapter 3 that for purposes of this study the extent to which those totals underestimate the actual frequency with which the eight offences occur is not a crucial problem. Unreported or unrecorded offences are of importance only to the extent that they vary systematically so that "each year we dip deeper into the well of criminal behaviour to fill the tank of criminal statistics a little higher" (Morris and Hawkins, 1970, p. 34). If that is the case, then the trends that have been described are largely spurious. The evidence from other countries suggests that, at least for the indicators selected, such concern is overstated. Data are available on the two most important potential systematic biases in the crime statistics – changes in the resources and the procedures of the Garda Siochana – and it is useful to pause here and consider the extent to which the trends we examined reflect such a bias. Did police resources and police organisation vary over time in a manner likely to have artifically induced the mid-1960s break in the crime series and the levelling off observed for some indicators in the early 1970s?

Changes in police resources and in police efficiency are readily gauged. In Table 2 the trends in annual strength and budget of the Garda Siochana are traced. The size of the force declined between 1951 and 1961, though only slightly, and remained constant thereafter until about 1971. Over the next five years the force expanded from 6,612 gardai at all ranks to 8,419, an increase of 27.3 per cent (*Statistical Abstract of Ireland*, various issues). This pattern is mirrored in the data on police expenditure. On balance, the evidence linking offence levels to the availability of resources is weak: over periods of sustained increases in the mid-1960s, garda resources did not vary. The overall correlation between the number of gardai and linear trend is .46.

It is possible to question the extent to which the growing garda manpower and budget shown in Table 2 actually translated into a greater garda presence in the terms likely to be relevant to this study. By the early 1970s, security duties associated with Northern Ireland represented a substantial burden on the force, one that expanded in later years. The information with which it would be possible to assess the size of the diversion of resources that took place is not available. However, it is highly unlikely that after 1970 there were substantial increases in the number of gardai assigned to individual stations, particularly in Dublin.

The impact of changes in the organisation of the Garda Siochana, unlike those in resources, were concentrated in the mid-1960s. During those years the Templemore Training Centre was opened, and many of the smaller rural stations disappeared in the course of consolidation. Motorised patrols in the cities replaced gardai on foot, the technical and communication supports of modern policing were imported, all within a policy of upgrading the force. It was also a period in which a concerted effort began to enlist public support for

Table 2: *Personnel and budget of the Garda Siochana, 1951–75*

	Garda stations	Garda strength	Expenditure*	
			Actual	At constant (1961) prices
1951	810	6,904	£3,032,031	£4,176,926
1961	758	6,612	5,639,610	5,639,610
1962	754	6,531	6,135,409	5,888,108
1963	749	6,401	7,568,430	7,086,545
1964	746	6,452	6,323,925	5,547,303
1965	745	6,568	8,441,530	7,052,239
1966	742	6,545	8,671,320	7,032,701
1967	741	6,536	9,763,572	7,675,764
1968	740	6,546	9,702,591	7,284,227
1969	719	6,543	9,970,858	6,967,755
1970	703	6,532	11,816,902	7,633,658
1971	697	6,612	14,723,924	8,727,874
1972	697	6,961	16,941,994	9,247,813
1973	700	7,794	22,620,279	11,079,697
1974	700	7,990	29,451,953	12,355,453
1975	700	8,419	52,135,676	18,065,030

Source: *Statistical Abstract of Ireland* and *Appropriation Accounts*
* From 1961 to 1974 expenditure data are for the fiscal year ending on 31 March of the year listed. Data for 1975 are for the calendar year. The £28,319,134 expended between 1 April 1974 and 31 December 1974 is not included in the table.

the gardai, with "Garda Patrol" becoming a regular programme on RTE in 1965. This emphasis emerges for the first time in the 1966 *Report on Crime*, which includes a section "Summary of Crime Prevention Activity" reporting on programmes aimed specifically at breaking and entering offences such as burglary. Given such a change in emphasis within the force and the growing technical competence of the gardai during the mid-1960s, it is certainly possible that despite the failure to effectively increase garda strength in those years the average garda became more efficient. That efficiency could plausibly have translated into a greater success in rooting out crime, both directly and indirectly through an increase in public confidence in the gardai. If so, it was a success that was rewarded by an increase in the crime statistics.

Changes in garda procedures or in garda efficiency would most likely be manifest in an improving detection rate. A detection occurs whenever the gardai are convinced that they have either apprehended or identified the individual(s) responsible for an offence. Table 3 provides the national-level detection rates for the eight offences being considered. Overall, there is little evidence that a substantial change occurred in the rates prior to 1970. Between 1969 and 1970 the detection rate declined precipitously for housebreaking, shopbreaking, larceny from vehicles, and robbery. Assault and receiving maintain stable levels of detections throughout, while for larceny of vehicles and for pedal cycle larceny a basic shift can be identified some years prior to the equivalent change in the other property offences. Therefore, given that major changes in detection rates do not coincide with those for offence levels, neither changing police methods nor resources are persuasive alternative explanations for the trends observed in Figures 1 through 6.

Changes in the liberality of public co-operation with the gardai or in the incentives to the public for reporting crimes are less easily measured. Certainly, the use made of the "999" emergency service has dramatically increased: there were 66,000 emergency telephone calls to the gardai in Dublin during 1967 and 115,000 such calls in 1975 (Report of the Commissioner of the Garda Siochana on crime, 1967; 1975). Also, as the seriousness of burglary has increased (though only slightly), so has the incentive to report offences to the gardai, if only to satisfy the requirements of insurance companies. The average value of stolen property in burglaries was £171.50 in 1975. But what evidence is available suggests that the trends in burglary have throughout reflected the incidents in which more than a token loss was sustained. Indeed, it was largely for this reason that housebreaking and shopbreaking were included as indicators. It does not seem to me reasonable to conclude that the post-1964 increase reflects a greater willingness to report breaking and entering offences. For assault, and for the minor property offences, the possibility is more real: McClintock (1963) attributes a substantial part of the increase in the number of known violent crimes in London between 1950 and 1960 to a diminishing public tolerance of interpersonal violence. Similarly, the tolerance by business firms of petty larceny declines as the losses involved come to be seen as a threat to profits. It is generally the case that efforts at "crime prevention" increase the crime rate. To the extent that shops undertake to provide their own security staff, for example, more offences will become known: petty larceny and like offences only become "known" if someone takes an interest in securing an arrest. If places of business become more vigilant and more likely to seek a prosecution, a crime wave can result. It is for that reason that petty larceny is excluded from the consideration of crime trends.

Table 3: *National detection rates 1951–1975*

				Offence category				
Year	Assault	Housebreaking	Shopbreaking	Larceny from vehicles	Robbery	Receiving	Larceny of vehicles	Pedal cycle larceny
	per cent	per cent	per cent	per cent	per cent	per cent	per cent	per cent
1951	94.5	74.6	68.4	30.0	62.5	100.0	76.2	24.1
1952	97.0	69.4	63.3	32.0	56.5	100.0	68.2	18.5
1953	97.8	71.4	67.4	36.0	52.8	100.0	44.1	20.7
1954	96.9	76.0	72.7	44.4	58.3	100.0	40.7	26.6
1955	96.1	83.6	72.5	40.1	78.0	100.0	44.8	20.7
1956	98.1	78.5	75.1	37.2	66.7	99.5	50.0	24.1
1957	98.2	79.0	71.0	35.3	69.7	99.4	44.7	16.8
1958	97.8	77.7	69.5	31.5	70.5	99.5	56.7	15.9
1959	97.1	73.7	66.5	35.2	69.5	98.6	75.0	14.4
1960	97.3	81.7	71.9	43.1	74.6	99.6	73.3	22.5
1961	97.8	80.0	73.9	48.7	73.8	98.9	63.8	31.1
1962	96.7	76.1	72.9	49.9	76.9	99.6	54.8	28.0
1963	98.8	78.9	72.2	45.5	73.8	100.0	59.1	27.8
1964	95.9	75.7	69.2	50.4	85.5	98.6	50.0	17.8
1965	96.8	78.9	71.4	54.2	75.3	99.7	48.8	25.9
1966	94.9	75.7	69.7	47.0	83.6	99.6	41.4	22.2
1967	95.5	71.4	66.7	46.6	75.6	100.0	42.0	21.5
1968	94.9	66.9	66.3	45.3	76.2	99.7	37.4	14.9
1969	95.5	63.0	64.7	48.1	79.6	99.7	28.7	13.0
1970	93.7	51.4	52.5	29.4	64.7	99.7	27.8	11.0
1971	93.0	50.5	48.1	25.9	47.5	100.0	22.8	7.6
1972	92.5	46.8	45.1	25.3	47.9	100.0	26.6	7.2
1973	93.1	47.5	47.7	29.1	56.5	100.0	28.3	9.4
1974	91.5	49.7	50.3	34.1	49.5	100.0	29.9	5.2
1975	92.0	42.8	49.0	27.9	45.3	100.0	26.3	5.4

In sum, while the possibility remains that trends in known offences are influenced by factors extraneous to the level of crime in the community, I do not regard it as a barrier to drawing conclusions based on the nine indicators selected for this study.

A Statistical Analysis of National Crime Trends Graphic presentation of the relationships between variables is a necessary first step for most analyses – it provides a convenient overview of the relationships at issue and limits the possibility that the statistical approximations of the relationships will be misinterpreted. The second contribution is particularly important for the trends being examined here. It is clear from the preceding figures that it will be extremely difficult to obtain a single trend that can adequately describe the variation in levels of offences over the full 25 years. The difficulty is most pronounced for larceny of pedal cycles, which has a cyclical pattern, but it will be present for all nine indicators. In itself, the difficulty of deriving adequate mathematical representations of the relationship between offence levels and time for years of interest suggests that, in fact, we are confronted with several rather than one series.

Table 4 directly addresses that possibility. The trend identified for the years 1951 to 1963 is contrasted for each of the nine indicators with the trend obtained for the years 1964 to 1975. When the graphs of the trends were examined, it appeared that the mid-1960s marked a watershed for all the offence categories and for the value of property stolen in burglaries. Indeed, the differences observed between the trends before and after that point suggested structural changes in the series. The regression results reported in Table 4 represent a more precise assessment of the transformation that occurred.

Two sets of regression results are given. The first was derived from regressing each indicator on linear trend (a variable created by numbering the years from 1 to 25 in sequence), the standard expression of change through annual increases that remain at a constant amount. A second specification regressing the natural logarithm of each offence indicator on linear trend, was also used to allow for the possibility of a non-linear relationship. This is termed a semilog model. The alternative specification of a double-log model did not prove useful and the results so obtained are not reported.

Table 4 permits three comparisons for each specification of trend. The strength of the trend is given by the R^2 measure of the amount of the variance explained by trend alone. (Given the small number of observations, the coefficients used are R^2s adjusted for degrees of freedom). From the metric coefficients (unstandardised regression coefficients) the direction and nature of the relationship with trend is shown. Finally, the table also gives the Durbin-Watson test statistic measuring the presence of autocorrelation

Table 4: *Variance in crime indicators attributable to trend: Linear and semi-logarithmic regressions.*

| | 1951–1963 | | | | | | | | 1964–1975 | | | | | | | |
| | Linear | | | | Semi-logarithm | | | | Linear | | | | Semi-logarithm | | | |
	Constant	b	R̄²	D.W.	Constant	b	R̄²	D.W.	Constant	b	R̄²	D.W.	Constant	b	R̄²	D.W.
Assault	124.2	23.2	.877	(1.2)	5.0	.08	.908	(1.7)	400.7	62.5	.879	(1.3)	6.2	.08	.921	(1.7)
Housebreaking	958.6	26.5	.303	(1.4)	6.9	.02	.301	(1.3)	501.6	434.0	.956	(1.0)	7.1	.14	.983	(1.2)
Shopbreaking	1,187.0	59.1	.470	(1.5)	7.1	.04	.443	(1.5)	1,366.9	410.1	.919	(1.5)	7.6	.10	.955	(1.6)
Larceny from vehicles	1,220.4	15.1*	.000	(1.7)	7.1	.01*	.000	(1.7)	333.0	718.2	.877	(1.3)	7.3	.16	.910	(1.0)
Robbery	24.3	2.1	.317	(1.4)	3.2	.06	.398	(1.7)	−126.7	65.6	.841	(0.9)	3.6	.26	.933	(0.9)
Receiving	189.5	3.7	.032	(1.0)	5.2	.02*	.034	(1.1)	221.1	25.6	.808	(1.6)	5.5	.07	.844	(1.8)
Larceny of vehicles	11.3*	3.8	.583	(0.9)	2.9	.09	.679	(1.6)	−19.5	58.9	.666	(1.0)	4.2	.21	.816	(0.8)
Pedal cycle larceny	2,441.6	−9.9	.000	(1.0)	7.8	.00*	.000	(0.9)	1,819.9	75.0	.344	(1.7)	7.5	.03	.328	(1.7)
Property value	28.9	−0.6	.140	(1.7)	3.4	−.02*	.130	(1.7)	26.7	1.9	.678	(1.9)	0.1*	.05	.716	(1.6)

*Denotes coefficients that are *less* than twice their standard error.

among disturbances. If such autocorrelation is present, the assumption made in ordinary least squares regression of error terms that are uncorrelated random variables is not fulfilled. In time-series analysis, it is frequently found that the value for one observation (year) is affected by the error term from the preceding year. Such positive autocorrelation is a warning that factors other than the relationship between the variables specifically included in the equation may be sufficiently active to make a satisfactory expression of the relationship of interest impossible.

Table 4 highlights the difference between the two time-periods. Prior to 1964, a clear upward trend is evident only for assault, while for two indicators – larceny of pedal cycles and value of stolen property – the tendency is towards a decrease. This contrasts sharply with the pattern between 1964 and 1975. Strong upward trends are evident in that period for all indicators except pedal cycle larceny. In the early period, trend explains 30.2 per cent of the variance in housebreaking levels and 47.0 per cent of the variance in shopbreaking. The comparable R^2s for the later period are 98.3 and 95.5 per cent (the coefficients noted for these offences are the ones with the most adequate Durbin-Watson results). In both periods, the importance of trend is less pronounced for indicators of the sophistication of property offences. But the differences within each period are insubstantial in comparison with the differences between periods. It is clear that for property offences the sustained series of increases commenced in 1964. The one anomaly is larceny of vehicles, which is influenced by trend in the 1950s nearly as much as in the 1970s. This suggests that a pattern similar to that identified by Mansfield *et al.* (1974) in Norway and the United States is operative in Ireland – substantial increases in offence levels are recorded in the initial period of scarcity of automobiles, followed after a saturation point is reached by a second upsurge, corresponding to an increase in larcenies by juveniles in periods of mass availability of automobiles.

Most of the Durbin-Watson statistics fall within or exceed the lower and upper bounds for rejecting the null hypothesis of positive autocorrelation. At the five per cent level, those bounds are 1.08 and 1.36 with 15 observations (Theil, 1971, p. 724). For the numbers of observations used in Table 4, the appropriate bounds will be slightly lower. For the most part, the tests for autocorrelation do not suggest that log-linear relationships are more adequate than are the standard linear specifications. However, in the 1951–1963 period, the logarithm approach is preferable for assault, robbery, and larceny of motor vehicles; in the later period this is true only for assault.

In sum, the regression results shown in Table 4 support the existence of a break in the nine statistical series being examined. As will be seen in Table 7, even for assault it is not possible to use a single trend measure to represent the full 25-year period. Therefore, it is reasonable to conclude that it is necessary to treat the mid-1960s as the crucial point in the transformation of Irish crime patterns.

The divergence of the post-1964 movements in the crime indicators from that which obtained in the earlier period is so striking for most offences as to be self-evident from the charts. A formal statistical test is available, however, by which the acuteness of our vision can be confirmed. The Chow test (1960) allows us to compare the null hypothesis of a stable relationship over the full 25 years between the indicator and time (in other words, the trend) for each offence with the hypothesised 1963/64 break in the series. To carry out the test, the time-period was subdivided into 1951–63 and 1964–75, and the sum of squares of the residuals from regression estimates in the two sub-periods compared with that found for the full 25-year period. When applied to the nine indicators, the null hypothesis was rejected at the .001 level for all indicators except pedal cycle larceny (and when the logarithms of the indicators were used, at the .05 level for all but pedal cycle larceny and assault). Therefore, the appropriate statistical expression of the crime indicator trends from 1951 to 1975 is that of a structural change (or shift in some texts) that can plausibly be located in 1963/64. There is no single overarching trend for those 25 years.[10]

This discrepancy between the trends found for 1951–1963 and those found for the post-1964 period has important implications. A strong upward linear trend, if equally present in all the indicators of crime, will produce a cohesive pattern of change to characterise that time-period. This is true of the 1964–1975 period. Such a pattern implies, but does not establish, that the various indicators are responding in a roughly comparable manner to a common set of socio-economic forces. The diversity of trends in the pre-1964 period and the homogeneity that obtains subsequently, therefore, sharply differentiates the two periods. But it must be stressed that the assertion of a common pattern of change cannot rest only on the presence of a shared linear trend. That trend must be supplemented by evidence that the indicators also share a pattern of movement around the trend line: when one indicator exceeds the level anticipated by trend, so should the other offence indicators.

Table 5 examines separately the intercorrelations among indicators for the two periods. The table presents for each period zero-order correlations based on offence levels which are contrasted with correlations between residuals.

---

[10]Tests are available for estimating the point at which a structural shift occurs without making any *a priori* decisions as to its location (see Goldfield and Quandt, 1973), but the issue here is the merits of a specific point in time.

Table 5: *Intercorrelations among crime indicators, by time period**

				1951 to 1975					
	1	2	3	4	5	6	7	8	9
1 Assault	1.0	.93	.93	.89	.88	.94	.85	.05	.80
2 Housebreaking	−.19	1.0	.99	.98	.96	.92	.91	.23	.84
3 Shopbreaking	−.37	.89	1.0	.98	.92	.90	.90	.22	.86
4 Larceny from vehicles	−.24	.94	.87	1.0	.95	.90	.96	.21	.84
5 Robbery	−.07	.86	.62	.82	.0	.90	.90	.19	.75
6 Receiving	.00	.49	.47	.50	.37	1.0	.88	.04	.81
7 Larceny of vehicles	−.08	.69	.65	.78	.54	.35	1.0	.11	.78
8 Pedal cycle larceny	−.45	.52	.55	.44	.46	−.00	.07	1.0	.06
9 Property value	−.05	.66	.63	.69	.40	.44	.66	.01	1.0

				1951 to 1963					
	1	2	3	4	5	6	7	8	9
1 Assault	1.0	.54	.66	.18	.48	.38	.87	−.21	−.33
2 Housebreaking	−.21	1.0	.88	.76	.72	.23	.59	.58	−.14
3 Shopbreaking	−.34	.79	1.0	.69	.50	.36	.75	.33	−.17
4 Larceny from vehicles	−.26	.78	.72	1.0	.52	.16	.30	.67	.06
5 Robbery	−.07	.54	.06	.44	1.0	−.00	.24	.58	−.49
6 Receiving	−.11	.12	.31	.16	−.32	1.0	.28	−.20	.17
7 Larceny of vehicles	.28	.26	.38	−.16	−.33	−.11	1.0	−.20	−.01
8 Pedal cycle larceny	−.39	.77	.54	.66	.71	−.12	−.12	1.0	−.22
9 Property value	.12	.21	.25	.27	−.25	.28	.66	−.29	1.0

				1964 to 1975					
	1	2	3	4	5	6	7	8	9
1 Assault	1.0	.93	.87	.84	.92	.94	.72	.53	.69
2 Housebreaking	−.53	1.0	.99	.96	.95	.89	.83	.68	.80
3 Shopbreaking	−.85	.81	1.0	.97	.91	.82	.82	.72	.84
4 Larceny from vehicles	−.60	.88	.75	1.0	.92	.85	.93	.63	.78
5 Robbery	.15	.39	−.00	.47	1.0	.92	.84	.52	.67
6 Receiving	.41	.03	−.40	.09	.56	1.0	.81	.45	.67
7 Larceny of vehicles	−.39	.67	.42	.87	.42	.23	1.0	.44	.65
8 Pedal cycle larceny	−.56	.29	.55	.15	−.30	−.31	−.13	1.0	.60
9 Property value	−.56	.24	.48	.22	−.31	−.37	.17	.19	1.0

*Coefficients above the diagonal in each matrix are zero-order correlations based on levels of known offences; coefficients below the diagonal are correlations based on the residuals derived from regressing each offence category against trend, with trend represented by a log curve.

The correlations based on levels, which are presented above the diagonal in each matrix, can be readily predicted from the results given in Table 4. However, the correlations between residuals, representing the strength of relationships after de-trending, are not straightforward. They are a more stringent test for the extent of cohesiveness. In all instances, the trend removed was that specified by a log curve. That specification was not equally satisfactory for all indicators, but if the results of the de-trending are to be interpretable, it is necessary to apply the same procedure throughout.

The de-trending of the relationships between crime indicators is accomplished by regressing each crime indicator on time (the trend). By taking the residual, which is the difference between what the trend predicts and what was recorded in the garda statistics, a measure is obtained of that indicator's movement around its trend line. When the residuals of two indicators, say, housebreaking and robbery, are correlated, the resulting coefficient expresses the strength of their de-trended relationship: whether the fluctuations around the linear trend are similar for the two indicators. An example may help explain the nature of the de-trending. If over a 25-year period the number of robberies increases from 1,000 to 3,500, the linear trend will assume that each annual increase over the period was about 100 additional robberies, with a prediction that the number of robberies in the second year was 1,100. If the actual number recorded was 1,230, the residual would be +130, meaning that there were 130 more robberies in that year than would be predicted on the basis of the 25-year trend.

As anticipated, the intercorrelations in Table 5 are weak in the 1951–1963 period and strong in the 1964–1975 period. In the earlier period, 10 of the 36 coefficients are negative; there are no negative correlations for the post-1964 years. Further, in all but three instances, the correlation for the later period exceeds the equivalent coefficient from the years 1951–1963. The basic difference conceals several interesting features of the two periods. When the intercorrelations among indicators of sophistication and among major property offences are examined, the cohesiveness in the later period and the disjointedness of the early period are highlighted. The level of receiving offences and the value of stolen property, which correlate at .17 in the period before 1964, have a correlation of .67 in the second period. Both indicators in the first period have either negative or weak positive relationships to other crime variables.

Examining the de-trended relationship, however, makes the contrast between the periods less emphatic. By the more stringent standard of common movement around trend, the major property offences evince substantial covariation in both periods, while the relationship between those offences and the indicators of sophistication and organisation is tentative both for

1951–1963 and for 1964–1975. This blurs the distinctions that emerge when trend is retained in the relationships. But distinctions remain. In particular, the forms of larceny dependent on motor vehicles have in the post-1964 period a stronger interrelationship with each other and stronger connections to other major property offences than in the preceding years.

Taken together, Tables 4 and 5, along with the Chow tests, demonstrate that the offence indicators except pedal cycle larceny underwent a structural change in about 1964; it is, therefore, not particularly meaningful to analyse the trend over the full 25 years as if it were one series. The results in Table 5 limit the interpretations that can be placed on the implications of those breaks: in neither period were the intercorrelations employing de-trended indicators such as to suggest a common movement in response to socio-economic conditions. However, evidence was found that in the later years major property offences, and especially those involving motor vehicles, were closely linked. This finding directs our attention to changes in the availability and nature of property that occurred in the mid-1960s, a theme that will be pursued in the next section of this chapter.

The Abundance of Property and the Crime Rate

Over the quarter century being studied here, both the level of recorded crime and the amount of property have grown considerably. This section attempts to systematically examine the relationship between opportunity in the form of property and the degree to which individuals avail of that opportunity through illegal means.

The first approach to quantifying that relationship establishes a surrogate for the value of all stealable property. Annual figures on the total value of personal expenditure on consumers' goods and services are used as a base by which the real growth in property loss from burglary can be tracked. Table 6 reports the results of this effort. The main indicator is the ratio of the value of stolen property to the total value of consumer expenditure. To facilitate the evaluation of the changes in that ratio, the 1951 ratio has been set equal to 100.0 and the ratios for all other years expressed as index numbers.

Table 6 confirms that the seriousness of property crime has increased since the mid-1960s. As a proportion of all property purchased that year in Ireland, the amount stolen through burglary has increased nearly five-fold over the 25 years included in the table. Until 1966, however, no increase at all in the ratio is registered: there is considerable variability in the ratio, but nowhere does it rise to a level greater than the 1951 figure. This changes dramatically in 1966, and the upward movement continues through 1970. Thereafter, with the exception of 1975, a new level of about three times the 1951 one has been established.

Index numbers are also used to plot separately the increases registered for the two components of the ratio. At constant prices, the value of stolen property in 1975 is 33 times as great as the value present at the start of the series. Given this huge increase in the amount of property taken through burglary, the approximately seven-fold increase in the total value of consumers' expenditure results in a substantially greater proportion of all property being removed through means that violate the criminal law. As would be expected, consumers' expenditure grows steadily across the 25 years; the rate of increase, however, itself rises in the mid-1960s and after. A very different pattern is present for the value of stolen property. For that index, the changes closely resemble those found for the levels of the two types of burglary. A permanent change takes place in the mid-1960s, with little increase in the property value prior to that point and very rapid increases after it.

Table 6 suggests that about 1964 a basic transformation occurred in the seriousness of loss sustained through property crime. Before 1964 there is no evidence that property crime is increasing systematically in response to the opportunities available. This is reversed in the years after 1964, where the annual increases are so large as to more than merely compensate for the growing opportunities – more advantage is being taken of all available opportunities. This also probably reflects a limitation in the approximation being used for opportunity. The use of annual data on consumer spending does not adequately represent the increases that are taking place in the stock of stealable objects and of cash. Consumers' expenditure is a *flow* that is not a firm indication in the accumulation of a *stock* of goods, and it is the stock present in a year that is the real indicator of opportunity. Still, consumers' expenditure does supply a useful yardstick with which the growth over time of property crime can be measured.

A more precise measure of the relationship between property availability and crime levels can be obtained if the focus is narrowed to the offence of motor vehicle larceny. For that offence, it is possible to trace changes in abundance, changes that Gould (1971) and Mansfield *et al* (1974) argue govern the market conditions to which amateur and professional car thieves respond. They argue, and produce data from the United States and Norway which confirms that laws of supply and demand act to establish a clear sequencing in the trends for the level of motor vehicle larceny. As the *per capita* rate of car ownership first begins to rise from a level of scarcity toward nearly universal car ownership, there is a corresponding rapid and sustained increase in the level of larceny, the vehicles being supplied by "professional" car thieves. Demand expressed through the illicit market rises until a saturation point is reached, with most households being car owners, creating a sequence in

Table 6: *Change indices for 1951–75: personal expenditure on consumer goods, value of property stolen in burglary, and the ratio of property value to personal expenditure.*

Year	Ratio	Property stolen	Personal expenditure
1951	100.0	100.0	100.0
1952	88.6	92.1	103.9
1953	95.6	107.5	112.4
1954	56.8	65.2	114.8
1955	64.9	80.3	123.8
1956	62.3	77.3	124.0
1957	73.3	93.0	126.8
1958	79.1	107.0	135.3
1959	89.0	122.2	137.3
1960	50.1	72.9	145.5
1961	59.5	91.3	153.4
1962	98.1	162.0	165.1
1963	85.9	151.5	176.2
1964	96.5	189.7	196.5
1965	99.6	206.1	206.9
1966	118.2	259.1	219.1
1967	144.9	339.1	234.0
1968	187.7	501.1	267.0
1969	204.2	619.3	303.2
1970	338.6	1,113.5	328.9
1971	279.9	1,036.4	370.3
1972	288.3	1,233.2	477.7
1973	301.3	1,522.0	505.2
1974	312.6	1,864.2	596.4
1975	472.9	3,333.1	704.9

Sources: *National Income and Expenditure*, 1976 and earlier editions, and the *Report on Crime*, various issues.

which the level of larceny first peaks and then declines. Ultimately, a second upward trend in motor vehicle larcenies emerges, this time in response to the entry into the market of "amateur" car thieves, mainly juveniles, who become the dominant force in the illicit market.

Figure 7 replicates with Irish data covering the years 1951 to 1975 the plot of the relationship specified by Mansfield *et al.* (1974, p. 469) between motor vehicle larcenies per 100,000 population and motor vehicle registrations per 1,000 population. The outlines of the first "peak" they anticipate and find in Norwegian data for the 1965 to 1967 period is also clearly present in the Irish data, though for Ireland the initial response to increased availability is more deliberate than was the case in Norway. At the highest level of availability in Norway (230 vehicles per 1,000 population) the larceny level is at a point parallelled in Figure 7 at about 140 vehicles per 1,000 population. Data from the United States, however, reporting substantially higher *per capita* vehicle registrations, continues the downward trend and then produces a sustained upward movement that is continuing at levels of 460 vehicles per 1,000 population.

The plausibility of the replication is enhanced by the extent to which the levels of abundance at which the initial upward trend commenced, coincide for the two countries. This occurred for both Norway and Ireland when there were about 100 vehicles per 1,000 population. However, though the comparison may be plausible, it remains inexact.

The transformation in Irish crime patterns that has been identified appears to have coincided with the accumulation of a stock of valuable property. That build-up was completed around the mid-1960s, and it is from that point that the trends for crime in Ireland depart from their traditional pattern. This is in accord with an explanation based on changing opportunities and does provide a link between general structural change and the level and pattern of crime. It must be stressed, however, that such an explanation leaves unanswered a vital question: why do people take advantage of the new opportunities for criminal activity?

Economic Conditions and Crime

Given the configurations found for changes in offence levels between 1951 and 1975, it is unlikely that economic cycles had a major role in shaping the observed trends. In particular, it is not possible for changes in unemployment levels or like variables to have engineered the break evident in most series, nor can they be held responsible for the rapid growth in the late 1960s. But it remains possible that there is a relationship between economic conditions and crime that merits elucidation, one that is relevant to the claims of the social disorganisation perspective.

There is a further reason for examining that relationship. The time-series analyses thus far have not satisfactorily represented the trend for the offence indicators. When the 25 years are examined, the Durbin–Watson statistics lead to the rejection of every specification used for the changes in offence levels. The auto-correlation for all equations is severe, with error terms strongly interdependent, and both regression coefficients and significance tests are therefore unreliable. Auto-correlated disturbances generally stem

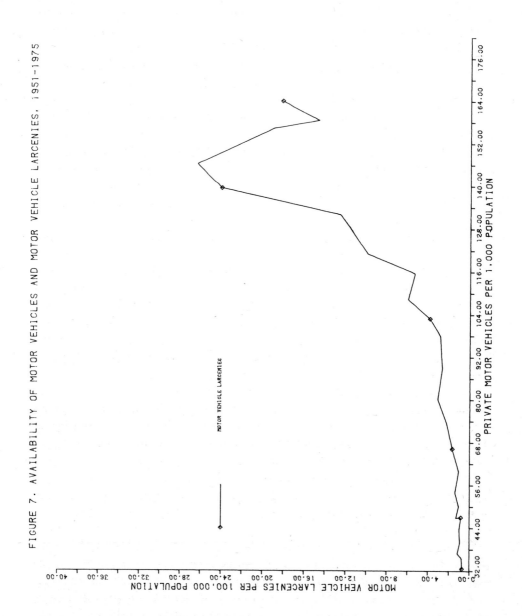

FIGURE 7. AVAILABILITY OF MOTOR VEHICLES AND MOTOR VEHICLE LARCENIES, 1951-1975

either from mis-specification of the relationship between variables or the omission from the equation of certain factors systematically related to the dependent variable. Since alternative specifications of the relationship between time and offence level have proved unrewarding, it is possible that including economic conditions may produce more satisfactory expressions of the trend in crime over the full time-period.

Table 7 regresses each of the nine indicators on two economic variables: the non-agricultural unemployment rate (as given in *The Trend of Employment and Unemployment*, various issues), and the ratio of actual Gross National Product to the level of GNP expected from its trend (taken from Walsh, 1978), a measure of economic growth. Both economic variables are lagged in all equations, a procedure that uses economic conditions in, say, 1974 to predict the level of crime in 1975. The standard justification for introducing a lag into a relationship is that an interval is necessary before the impact of macro-economic changes filters down to the living circumstances of individuals. In the present study, lagged variables have an additional virtue: because of the use by the gardai between 1958 and 1974 of crime reporting years that commenced on 1 October, in the absence of a lag I would, in effect, be predicting crime levels from the subsequent economic climate.

Three equations are reported for each crime indicator. The first equation regresses offence level on trend, the second equation adds unemployment rate to trend, and the third equation includes trend and both economic variables. Unemployment data did not become available as a consistent time-series until 1954 and this, along with the need to drop one year to allow for the lag, results in the years 1955 to 1975 forming the observations for the analysis.

For assault and for receiving, the straightforward time-offence level relationship is acceptable. The Durbin-Watson statistics are unsatisfactory for all other indicators. However, for those seven indicators, the addition of economic variables into the equation raises the Durbin-Watson statistic to acceptable levels and generally increases the amount of variance explained. Unemployment alone increases the explained variance in housebreaking by 6.5 per cent, in larceny from vehicles by 5.7 per cent, in robbery by 12.6 per cent, and in pedal cycle larceny by 48.6 per cent. The effects from change in GNP for these indicators are minor on explained variance, but that variable's addition to the equation is beneficial in terms of raising the Durbin-Watson. All of the relationships between unemployment and offence levels are positive: high levels of known offences tend to occur in periods of high unemployment. Growth in GNP, where the coefficient is statistically significant, is generally positive, except in the case of larceny of pedal cycles where the ratio increases the explained variance by 10 per cent through a negative relationship. It is intriguing, but probably inexplicable, that it should be the

Table 7: *The regression of offence-indicators on economic conditions and trend, 1955–75.*

Equation number	Log of offence category	Intercept	Trend	Unemployment rates	GNP ratio	$\bar{R}^2$	DW
1.1	Assault	5.35 (138.1)	.084 (27.1)			.971	1.54
1.2		5.57 (41.7)	.083 (28.2)	−.030 (1.7)		.973	1.77
1.3		5.11 (12.6)	.081 (26.2)	−.035 (2.0)	.005 (1.2)	.973	1.84
2.1	Housebreaking	6.56 (83.9)	.094 (15.1)			.911	.33
2.2		5.47 (37.3)	.098 (30.6)	.149 (7.8)		.976	1.04
2.3		4.09 (12.4)	.094 (37.0)	.134 (9.4)	.015 (4.4)	.987	1.64
3.1	Shopbreaking	6.99 (116.1)	.082 (17.0)			.929	1.00
3.2		6.42 (35.3)	.084 (20.9)	.076 (3.2)		.949	1.71
3.3		5.97 (10.7)	.082 (19.1)	.071 (2.9)	.005 (0.9)	.948	1.78
4.1	Larceny from vehicles	6.63 (55.8)	.112 (11.9)			.863	.47
4.2		5.34 (16.4)	.117 (16.4)	.176 (4.1)		.920	1.15
4.3		2.81 (3.4)	.109 (17.0)	.149 (4.1)	.028 (3.2)	.943	1.65
5.1	Robbery	2.91 (15.4)	.158 (10.5)			.831	.41
5.2		.230 (0.7)	.169 (22.4)	.365 (8.1)		.957	1.16
5.3		−2.83 (3.5)	.159 (25.7)	.332 (9.6)	.034 (4.0)	.974	1.62
6.1	Receiving stolen goods	5.06 (100.3)	.057 (14.2)			.901	2.05
6.2		4.97 (26.9)	.057 (14.2)	.012 (0.5)		.897	2.13
6.3		4.99 (8.6)	.057 (13.0)	.013 (0.5)	.000 (0.0)	.890	2.13
7.1	Larceny of vehicles	2.75 (19.6)	.185 (16.5)			.925	.93
7.2		2.32 (4.5)	.187 (16.7)	.058 (0.9)		.924	.99
7.3		−.80 (0.6)	.176 (16.2)	.025 (0.4)	.035 (2.3)	.936	1.34
8.1	Pedal cycle larceny	7.65 (71.9)	.007 (0.80)			.000	.86
8.2		6.42 (23.3)	.011 (1.9)	.168 (4.7)		.468	1.34
8.3		8.34 (11.3)	.018 (3.1)	.189 (5.9)	−.021 (2.8)	.586	1.97
9.1	Property value	2.93 (42.6)	.045 (8.2)			.749	1.33
9.2		2.90 (11.4)	.045 (8.1)	.005 (0.2)		.736	1.33
9.3		1.00 (1.5)	.039 (7.7)	−.015 (.5)	.021 (3.0)	.806	2.09

*Parentheses contain t-ratios for coefficients.

offence of pedal cycle larceny that evinces no relationship with linear trend and is the indicator with the clearest relationship to economic conditions.

Change in GNP produces statistically significant coefficients for larceny of motor vehicles and for the value of stolen property. Both relationships are positive. The addition of GNP growth into the equation increases the variance explained in property value by 6.5 per cent. That is, when the economy is expanding at a rate in excess of its trend, the value of stolen property tends also to be higher than would be the case otherwise.

For three offences – assault, receiving, and shopbreaking – neither economic variable appreciably improves the variance explained by trend on its own. It is worth noting, however, that unemployment has a negative relationship with assault.

Table 7 establishes a pattern linking economic conditions to crime. It is the pattern that would be anticipated: property crime is more prevalent in periods of high unemployment. The regression results are for the most part very encouraging, particularly given the improvements made to R^2 (explained variance) and the Durbin-Watson statistics that are in excess of the upper bound for rejecting the null hypothesis of autocorrelation (at the five per cent level). But it is necessary to retain perspective by emphasising the dominance throughout the table of the effect from trend, a movement toward higher levels that is not explained by the economic or social variables considered thus far. Unemployment and GNP change do not reduce the impact of trend, they merely augment the 80 per cent and higher levels of variance that trend "explains" for all indicators except pedal cycle larceny.

Finally, it should be noted that multicollinearity does not appear to be a problem in Table 7. Trend has a correlation of −.17 with unemployment and of .37 with the GNP ratio. The two economic variables correlate at .15.

Conclusions and Interpretation

Analysis of data on Irish crime trends supports, by and large, the assertion that increased crime rates are most usefully understood within the context of a society's social structural change. This emerged when three comparisons were made of trends between 1951 and 1975: property crimes involving quite different types of property were compared, person offences were compared with property offences, and indicators of change in prevalence were compared with indicators of offence seriousness.

Those comparisons were used to address two questions. First, it was necessary to ascertain if the trends present in the crime indicators responded to the main outlines of social structural change in an interpretable manner. In particular, the consistency in the trends was examined. The sequencing of crime trends was sufficiently consistent to justify a conclusion that in Ireland a "structural change" in criminal activity was one concomitant of the general break with Ireland's economic past that occurred in the early 1960s. That is, a watershed was reached, one that cannot be understood in terms of a process of gradual accommodation to change.

From the graphic and statistical analyses of the crime trends, the amount of increase, the nature of the trends, and the timing of the "take off" point all emerge clearly. The only reasonable description to give the changes recorded in the crime statistics over the 25 years is that of a structural break that occurred in the mid-1960s. There is little continuity between pre-1964 crime statistics and what occurred subsequently; a watershed was reached.

The increases recorded in the crime statistics, therefore, are in basic accord with a structural explanation of linking social change to crime. A social disorganisation approach to that link suggests, in my view, either a pattern of constant growth, and probably one that commenced in the 1950s, or in some formulations, cyclical fluctuation in response to changing economic fortunes. Neither description is applicable to the trends in property crime. For assault, however, a growth curve beginning in the early 1950s could be identified.

Having identified the basic consistencies in the data and suggested that they support the general approach taken by the structural perspective, it remains to identify components of social structural change that were active in shaping the observed trends. While we cannot expect to establish causal relationships, some of the analyses presented in this chapter are certainly suggestive. For two types of property crime, burglary and larceny of motor vehicles, a connection can be shown between changes in the availability of the relevant types of property and the incidence of offences.

Chapter 5

Urban-Rural Differences in Crime Trends

Introduction

In our imagery of crime, dangerous places are urban places. Certain metropolitan milieus have become, in literature and in the visual arts, standard representations of menace and lawlessness. It is perhaps inevitable, therefore, that the substantial increases sustained in the level of recorded crime since the mid-1960s will be attributed to the cities and particularly to Dublin.

The accuracy of that perception is important in terms of what it can reveal about the nature of the growth in crime and what it suggests can, or ought, to be done as a matter of public policy. In both instances, the potential contribution comes from insight into the applicability to Ireland of experiences and lessons from elsewhere. The two main explanations for the impact of social change on crime, social disorganisation and structural theories, lead to contrasting expectations for Ireland as to the contributions urban and rural areas will make to national crime trends. That contrast can help us to identify the societal changes that were responsible for the substantial increases in the level of crime over the past quarter century. Further, geographic distribution is one aspect of the pattern of crime in Ireland, and if urban and rural trends were indeed dissimilar over those years, then that pattern inevitably altered. But the practical implications of urban-rural differences are sufficiently straightforward to require no elaboration. If something is to be done about a problem, it is a prerequisite to know where it is concentrated.

At present, it is reasonable to assume that our beliefs about the distribution of crime in Ireland primarily reflect what we know about the situation in other countries. The published garda crime statistics are not very informative about the location of offences. In the annual reports, there is a clear focus on the national picture. However, trends in the four traditional categories of indictable offences can be calculated separately for each garda division, (one of which is the Dublin Metropolitan Area) and for the city districts of Cork, Galway, Limerick and Waterford. It was necessary to supplement this published information, with data disaggregated into the nine specific indicators being used for this study, a process that proved feasible only for the 1964 to 1975 period. Therefore, this chapter compares the trends since 1964 that occurred in three types of areas: Dublin, the next four largest cities (Cork, Galway, Limerick, and Waterford combined), and the remainder of the country. Though crude, the comparisons so permitted do approximate the distinctions at issue when the impact of urbanism or urbanisation on crime is being discussed.

The link between this chapter and Chapter 2 derives from the contrasting roles that social disorganisation and structural perspectives attribute to the city. If the post-1964 substantial increases in the level of crime are viewed as the response to disorganisation, and, if as in other countries, that disorganisation is expressed most acutely in cities, then a disproportionate share of the rise in crime should have occurred in urban places. It was noted, however, that the relevance of the urbanisation experience in other countries to the Irish situation is questionable. When the social disorganisation approach is applied to Ireland in the 1951–1975 period the conditions that are highlighted as conducive to rising crime rates appear in rural rather than in urban areas. The severe dislocations experienced in the course of emigration during the 1950s were concentrated in small rural communities, while Dublin, like the Swiss cities studied by Clinard (1978), did not act as a magnet for the displaced rural poor. Though that role is more applicable to Dublin in the 1960s, perhaps supplemented by dislocations in some of the city's neighbourhoods, the force of the disorganisation argument is not impressive.

By departing from the urbanisation model implicit in the social disorganisation approach, Ireland is unlikely to have experienced the typical sequencing in which the post-1964 increases would commence in Dublin, only gradually being augmented by increasing crime rates in smaller urban places and then still later in rural districts. The concentration of crime in Dublin would in such a scenario have become more pronounced after the mid-1960s. That might have ultimately reversed, as conditions reached a "take off" point in other areas, but in the 1964–1975 period the predominance of Dublin in shaping the national trends seems inevitable.

It is inevitable, however, only to the extent that social change in Ireland conformed to the expectations of the social disorganisation approach. The departure from those expectations is significant, as is the distinctiveness of Ireland from the other atypical case, Switzerland (as described by Clinard, 1978). Certainly, Switzerland cannot provide a precedent for the suddenness and rapidity with which economic change intruded into and transformed Irish society.

A structural perspective seems preferable if the problem is so defined. It is likely that certain forms of structural change will tend to promote trends in crime that are indeed city-based, while other forms will create a truly national impact. Once the most important aspects of structural change in a period are identified, the susceptibility of various types of areas should become clear. And assistance in determining what those aspects are is more likely to be forthcoming from the writers I have labelled structural than from those in the social disorganisation tradition.

The distribution of "mobile" property, objects that are both valued and readily appropriated, is one factor that can be readily identified. The abruptness of the shift in crime trends found in the last chapter suggests that such changes might easily have overshot city boundaries and been manifested nationally. Certainly the idea of a gradual sequencing of adjustments to change, first in Dublin, then in other cities, and finally in the countryside seems implausible given the rapidity with which the changes occurred.

If that is the case, then the distribution of stealable property ought to have been fairly equitable in geographic terms. But simple availability is not sufficient. The response made to such property should also have been general, as opposed to contrasting urban and rural views.

It is possible to examine, albeit imprecisely, the distribution of some types of property. There is evidence that by the late 1960s car ownership rates for *counties* had substantially converged, though this was less true in the distribution of television sets (McCarthy and Ryan, 1976, pp. 271–272). In the course of the data analysis, account will be taken, where possible, of the availability of the relevant property. Changing beliefs about property, however, cannot be measured. What can be examined are the trends for the three area-types. To the extent that property crime is increasing at a similar pace across the three types, then the weight of evidence for a structural break in the level and pattern of crime becomes stronger. The effect of change was so great as to have been pervasive to the entire society. Or, put more precisely, that is the interpretation that seems most reasonable to me.

As in the preceding chapter, the interpretation of the trends for the nine indicators will be on comparing offences involving different types of property and on comparing property offences generally with assault. Such comparisons are complicated in the present chapter by the need to, at the same time, compare the trends for the three types of areas. The next section undertakes a detailed examination of the data on the distribution of property crime, deriving conclusions of the degree to which the incidence and organisation of such crimes have changed between 1964 and 1975 in the three area types. Each indicator will be taken separately and an assessment made; the same ground will be covered for offences against persons in a separate section. Assistance in the task of synthesising the various trends will be sought in a section using statistical analysis, while an attempt to reconcile the trends using the two perspectives will be left to a concluding section.

Offences Against Property

Burglary, subdivided into housebreaking and shopbreaking, once again begins the examination of trends in the eight crime indicators representing offences directed at the acquisition of property. Between 1964 and 1975, the number of housebreakings increased four-fold and the number of shopbreakings three-fold nationally. Figure 8 shows the trends in those 12 years separately for Dublin, the next four largest cities, and the non-urban areas. All three types of areas essentially replicate the national trends, registering substantial increases. Where 1964 levels are set equal to 100 and index numbers computed to represent the extent of increases, the 1975 housebreaking level stands at 487.0 in Dublin, 535.7 in the four-cities, and 325.2 in the non-urban areas. The corresponding index numbers for shopbreaking are 352.5, 305.3, and 274.9. Thus, the greatest increases were found in the urban areas, particularly for housebreaking.

The use of the actual numbers of known offences provides some useful perspective on what the trends in Figure 8 represent: 736 housebreakings and 1,089 shopbreakings were recorded in Dublin during 1964; 3,584 housebreakings and 3,839 shopbreakings in 1975. In the four-cities, the corresponding 1964 figures were 157 and 337; those for 1975 were 841 and 1,029. The remainder of the country was the location of 606 housebreakings and 846 shopbreakings in 1964 and in 1975 of 1,971 housebreakings and 2,326 shopbreakings.

A shift in the distribution of burglary, enhancing its predominantly urban emphasis, occurred between 1964 and 1975. This should not obscure the substantial increases registered in non-urban areas, or the basic consistency among area-types in the relationship between shopbreakings and housebreakings. It does, however, clarify the relative contribution to the national trends from different area-types. The impact by 1975 was to create marked differentials in the *per capita* incidence of burglary. Though the population bases being used are estimates, the following rates per 10,000 population can be offered. For housebreaking, the 1975 rates are 36.2 in Dublin, 23.8 in the four cities, and 10.8 in the non-urban areas. The corresponding rates for shopbreaking are 38.8, 29.1, and 12.8.

Given the diversity among burglary incidents, it is possible that the trends in each area-type represent increases in offences of quite different seriousness of loss and degree of organisation. As in the previous chapter, information on changes in the average value of property stolen in burglaries can be contrasted with the trends for offence levels. Table 8 shows the changing average value, expressed as constant (1964) prices. The comparisons between the three areas are interesting, though it is necessary to allow for greater susceptibility of the four-cities data to extreme scores. Indeed, the average fluctuates considerably for all areas, with a trend being most pronounced in the non-urban areas, in which the most substantial increase was recorded over the 12 years. In all areas, the losses are far from trivial. At current prices, the average losses in 1975 were £180.13 for Dublin, £124.24 for the four-cities, and £176.46 for the non-urban areas.

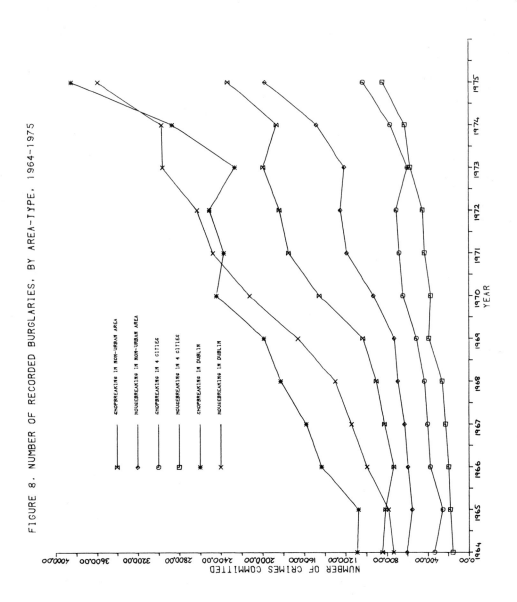

FIGURE 8. NUMBER OF RECORDED BURGLARIES, BY AREA-TYPE, 1964-1975

When the average loss is used as an indicator of the degree of organisation and effort involved in the burglaries, the greatest change clearly is in the non-urban areas. Only there has the average financial loss increased at the same pace as did the number of offences. The absence of a clear trend for urban areas suggests, perhaps, a greater diversity in participants and targets. One interpretation of the trend for non-urban areas is that there, over time, burglary has become more an enterprise of adults, and indeed has become more vocational than avocational, resulting in a sharp increase in the seriousness of the loss sustained. In 1964, the average loss in non-urban areas is one-half that in urban areas; there is no difference in 1975.

Table 8: *Average value of property stolen in burglaries*
(in constant-1964-prices)

Year	Dublin	Four-cities	Non-urban
1964	£43.80	£57.08	£22.56
1965	48.97	43.65	24.89
1966	48.63	26.71	29.77
1967	58.07	22.40	27.11
1968	65.90	43.94	38.91
1969	63.73	38.02	40.76
1970	87.65	28.19	57.42
1971	67.65	37.75	38.35
1972	64.81	33.97	50.36
1973	65.15	34.22	66.26
1974	65.39	27.38	61.36*
1975	71.14	49.07	69.69

*The £5,000,000 represented by the Beit Collection is omitted from the calculation.

Figure 8 and Table 8 present contradictory information on where to allocate the predominant weight in shaping the national trends. Urban areas clearly provided the major contribution to the growth since 1964 in the level of burglary, but the increase in the average loss appears to owe far more to the non-urban areas. The latter change is probably the more remarkable. All three area-types have clear upward trends in levels of offences; that consistency deserves as much, or more, attention as is given to the greater rate of increase in urban than in rural areas. Whatever factors drove those trends were apparently operative throughout the country. In all areas, the consistency in housebreaking and shopbreaking trends further suggests that specialisation in targets does not differentiate the changes recorded. This similarity is not present for the changes in the seriousness of burglary, at least as I have measured it. An upward trend is clearly identifiable only outside of the urban areas.

The trends in detection rates for burglary can also be used to examine the differences between urban and rural areas. Since the problems of identifying and apprehending suspects are presumably greater in urban areas, and given the lower levels of incidence in rural areas, it is reasonable to assume that the urban gardai would be less successful in obtaining detections. Also, the burden of the more substantial increases in offence levels found in cities might well in itself lead to a rapidly declining detection rate that would not be paralleled in non-urban areas.

Table 9 provides the relevant information. In all three areas, during the mid-1960s approximately three-fourths of housebreakings and over two-thirds of shopbreakings met the garda criteria for being considered solved. While the rate of detection begins to fall earlier in Dublin than elsewhere, at most points in time the rates are roughly equivalent across areas. Two years, however, require emphasis. Though the differences between areas in 1974 and 1975 are no larger than is typically the case, the ordering is contrary to expectations of experience in other countries or of common sense: in those two years, the detection rates in Dublin for both forms of burglary exceed those found in the other two areas.

The trends in detection rates for burglary are primarily noteworthy for the rough equivalence present among the types of areas. To the extent that differences do exist, they run contrary to the expectation of high rates in non-urban areas and low rates in urban areas. A partial explanation is the growing mobility of the population, making the transient as much, or more, a feature of the small city, town, or village as of the metropolis. A burglary committed by someone outside of their own locality is less likely to be detected. Together, the low detection rate and high average loss for burglaries in non-urban areas suggest, but do not establish, that many such offences are indeed committed by individuals visiting an area with that specific intention.

While not strictly a monotonic decrease, the trend in detection rates over time is clearly one of decline. It is a decline, however, effected not by gradual diminution but by a clear break in each series. The abruptness of that break, which occurred at the close of the decade, is marked: 74.2 per cent of all housebreakings reported in the non-urban areas during 1969 were detected; in 1970 only 58.7 per cent were so regarded. Re-examining Figure 8 suggests

Table 9: *Detection rates for burglaries*

	Housebreaking			Shopbreaking		
Year	Dublin	Four-cities	Non-urban	Dublin	Four-cities	Non-urban
	per cent	per cent	per cent	per cent	per cent	per cent
1964	73.4	80.3	77.2	69.7	71.5	67.6
1965	80.4	75.3	77.9	73.4	64.7	70.9
1966	71.0	76.3	83.2	68.1	63.7	75.8
1967	64.0	77.6	82.5	64.8	61.6	72.8
1968	64.6	63.6	72.6	66.4	63.4	67.6
1969	55.0	76.3	74.2	64.4	59.5	67.8
1970	47.8	54.0	58.7	50.4	52.3	56.2
1971	50.1	47.5	52.5	50.3	47.9	45.3
1972	46.1	54.3	45.6	45.0	48.2	44.1
1973	50.1	46.3	41.9	49.5	50.3	44.9
1974	53.1	44.4	45.0	54.0	47.3	45.9
1975	45.5	40.8	38.7	56.3	40.1	40.8

a connection between the sharp increases in levels of incidence and the rapid-ly diminishing detection rate: the number detected remains constant while the number known increases. For Dublin, this occurred both in 1968/1969 and in 1969/1970 for housebreakings. In the other areas, only the latter change is evident.

This pattern of an abrupt decline in the detection rate at the close of the 1960s was noted in discussing the national trends. The considerable diversion of garda resources to security duties at that time was doubtlessly a con-tributory factor. Though the amount of resources available to the gardai in-creased significantly during the 1970s, the real weight of that increase was not felt until after 1972. Assuming that in a given area-type there is a quota of an-nual detections that is more or less standard for a garda, the removal of a sub-stantial number of gardai from their ordinary duties could result in fewer detections overall. But such an explanation is unsatisfactory. As Reiss and Bordua (1967 p. 47) note: "No police department can know more crime than its resources make possible for it to know in that given period of time nor solve more than its resources make possible." If their argument is correct, then the impact of the declining resources for deployment to ordinary police work ought also to have been felt in the number of known offences. The number of gardai available obviously affects the probability that offences will be "discovered" in the course of patrolling; however, for less serious incidents the diminished availability of gardai to receive reports of crime from the public should also be reflected in the statistics. This does not appear to have been the case. On balance, though the role of increased security duties in the detection rates' abrupt decline was probably substantial, and particularly so in the limits imposed on investigatory work leading to a large number of of-fences being "solved" simultaneously, the decline also probably reflects movement within the force toward standardisation of procedures: the defini-tion of "detection" ceased to differ between urban and rural areas.

The evidence from burglary trends does not, by and large, support an as-sociation of the national trends primarily with urban areas. This is more a result of the ambiguity in the data than from a clear picture of equivalence between urban and rural areas. Over the 12 years, the distribution of burglary offences does shift toward a greater urban presence, but the trends in the average value of property stolen and in detections balance that tendency, precluding an association of the national trends with changes con-centrated within urban settings.

Another pair of offences, larceny of motor vehicles and larceny from unat-tended motor vehicles, can provide a basis for establishing the extent to which urban/rural differences in incidence of property crime trends are sensitive to the availability of property. Figure 9 gives the trends by type of area for

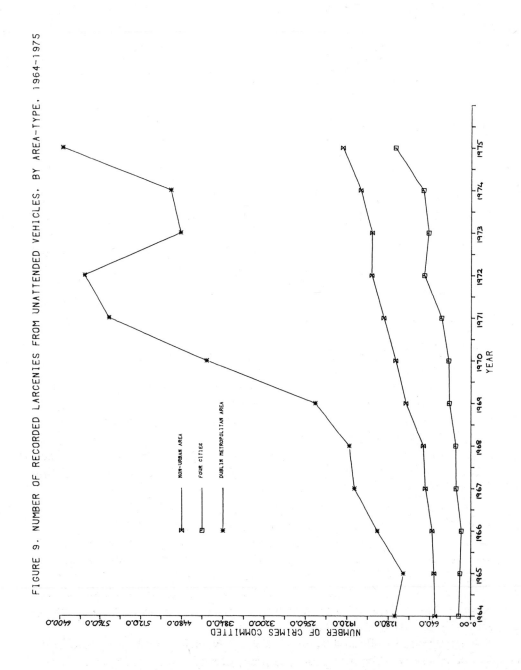

FIGURE 9. NUMBER OF RECORDED LARCENIES FROM UNATTENDED VEHICLES, BY AREA-TYPE, 1964-1975

larceny from unattended vehicles. The trends for all areas are of substantial increases. If the 1964 totals are taken as equal to 100, the magnitude of the increase over the time-period is evident from the 1975 index numbers: 536.1 for Dublin, 616.8 for the four-cities, and 353.3 for the non-urban areas. When 1975 rates based on the resident population, are computed for each area, the distribution of reported larcenies from vehicles even more strikingly differentiates urban and non-urban: the rates are 64.1 per 10,000 population in Dublin, 33.3 per 10,000 population in the four cities, and 10.9 per 10,000 population in the remainder of the country.

The differences in trends and in the *per capita* distribution of offences among types of areas do not have a straightforward association with levels of opportunity. The increase in the number of available vehicles proceeded at a roughly equivalent rate across the areas; the number of vehicles in 1975 was double the 1964 figure, the ratios being 1.95 for Dublin and 2.03 in both the four cities and the non-urban areas. As a result, the distribution of private motor vehicles among the area types remains stable throughout the 12 years, with about 29 per cent of all such vehicles in Dublin, just under 25 per cent in the counties in which the four cities are located, and nearly 47 per cent in what are termed here the non-urban areas.

Figure 10 formally introduces the availability of property as a basis for calculating property crime rates. For example, in 1975 the 6,347 reported larcenies from 148,718 private motor vehicles registered to residents of County Dublin, result in a rate of 42.7 larcenies per 1,000 vehicles. Rates are derived on the basis of vehicles registered to residents of the *counties* in which the cities of interest are located. The denominator for the non-urban areas, therefore, is the number of vehicles registered in the remaining 21 counties. By erring in the direction of being more inclusive for cities, some compensation is introduced for the discrepancy between the number of vehicles likely to be physically present in a city on a given day and the number of vehicles registered to residents of that city. Still, for Dublin and the four-cities, the denominators used in the rates probably understate the total number of vehicles physically present and thus available to enter the statistics as crime scenes.

Urban/non-urban differences are also clearly evident in the detection rates. Whatever year in Table 10 is examined, the lowest level of detections is in Dublin. While this is perhaps the most striking aspect of the detection rates, the sharply decreasing rates in the four-cities and in the non-urban areas are also noteworthy. So is the abrupt decline in detection rates between 1969 and 1970. In Dublin, the abrupt decline was associated with a marked increase in the number of known offences; this relationship was not evident for the four-cities or the non-urban areas.

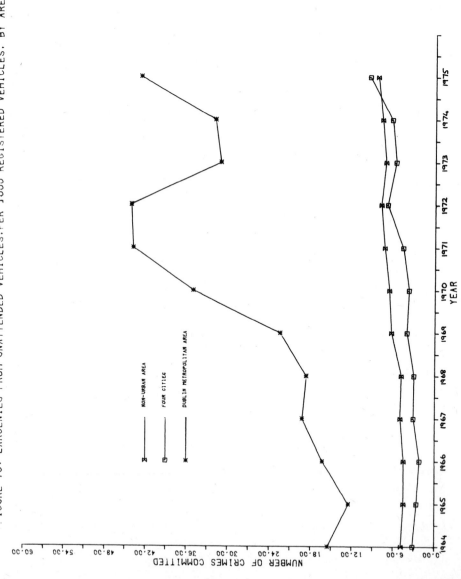

FIGURE 10. LARCENIES FROM UNATTENDED VEHICLES, PER 1000 REGISTERED VEHICLES, BY AREA-TYPE, 1964-1975

Despite some differences in the amount of the increase recorded over the 12 years, the consistency in the trends merits attention. The overall increase in the levels of larceny from vehicles is everywhere very substantial, with the four-cities experiencing the greatest change, followed by Dublin and then the non-urban areas. This ordering holds whether the number of recorded offences or rates per 1,000 vehicles are used. However, the extent of the increase is less awesome if the supply of vehicles is taken into account; when the 1964 rate is set to 100, the 1975 index numbers are 275.5 in Dublin, 306.5 in the four-cities, and 172.9 in the non-urban areas. The net impact of the upward trends, therefore, is to accentuate urban/rural differences. Simultaneously, differences between Dublin and the four-cities in levels of incidence narrow.

Table 10: *Detection rates for larcenies from motor vehicles*

Year	Dublin	Four-cities	Non-urban
	per cent	per cent	per cent
1964	33.6	63.4	81.2
1965	35.5	65.7	84.7
1966	29.4	72.9	82.2
1967	30.1	69.7	80.7
1968	30.4	72.1	74.4
1969	34.9	77.3	69.5
1970	18.2	54.1	61.0
1971	18.5	42.2	50.7
1972	17.9	38.1	48.4
1973	22.7	35.1	44.9
1974	31.7	29.0	42.8
1975	26.4	24.6	34.6

The trends for larceny of motor vehicles, shown in Figure 11, approximate those found for larceny from unattended vehicles. Disparities between Dublin and other areas persist and indeed increase over the 12 years, though the trends are less clearly linear than those found in Figure 10. There is a clear break in each series, with levels in the mid-1970s exceeding those registered during the mid-1960s through an abrupt shift that occurs between 1970 and 1971. In the two types of urban areas, the highest offence levels are recorded in 1972; in the non-urban areas, the peak occurs in 1973. Thereafter, the descent is rapid, with 1975 levels for the urban areas in particular substantially

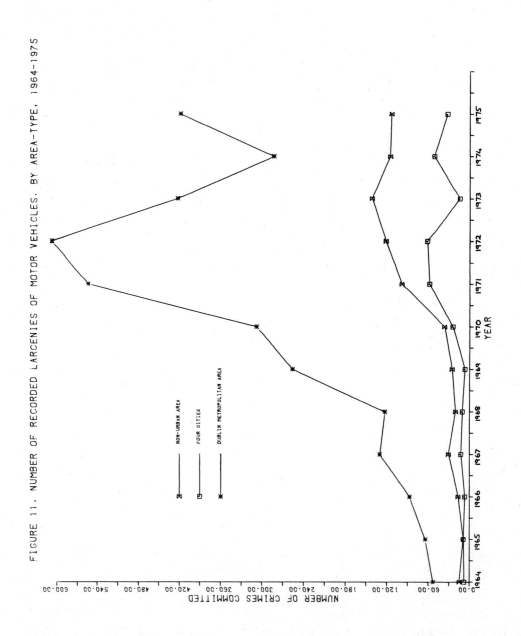

FIGURE 11. NUMBER OF RECORDED LARCENIES OF MOTOR VEHICLES, BY AREA-TYPE, 1964-1975

lower than those prevailing earlier in the decade. Table 11 examines the same trends using rates per 10,000 private motor vehicles registered in each type of area. The use of rates rather than offence levels does not alter the generalisations given above. With the 1964 levels set to 100, the 1975 index numbers are: Dublin, 790.6; four-cities, 412.5; and non-urban 760.0.

The trends in detection rates for motor vehicle larceny shown in Table 12 establish greater differences between Dublin and other areas than did comparable data for larcenies from vehicles. Also, the movement toward lower detection rates is less consistent than was the case for other property offences. Over time, motor vehicle larceny in Dublin becomes more prevalent and less susceptible to detection than in other areas.

The marked differentials between urban and rural trends and the apparent existence of a saturation point in the level of offences, which can be identified in all three areas, makes the offence of larceny of vehicles distinctive. The property sought through burglary is non-specific; the range of portable and marketable property delimits the possibilities. Similarly, though larcenies from motor vehicles perforce require that a supply of vehicles be present, the property sought is indeterminate. Where the vehicle itself is the target, the levels of theft are likely to correspond to the laws of supply and demand (Mansfield *et al.*, 1974). Though the levels of motor vehicle larceny are far higher in Dublin, the trends in all three types of area conform to the basic outline suggested by Mansfield and his colleagues: as *per capita* car ownership rises toward abundance, offence levels are initially a direct reflection of increasing availability. Eventually, however, a level is reached which the demand for vehicles through the illegal market declines sufficiently to create a downward trend. To that extent, the trends across the three area-types are similar.

The influence of the form of property on trends in offence levels and detection rates is evident in the data describing pedal cycle larceny. At least until the recent introduction of expensive racing models, pedal cycle larceny was unlikely, in a period of substantial availability of motor vehicles, to fluctuate in response to a well-defined illicit market. Figure 12 reveals a sharp contrast between Dublin and other areas in trends for 1964 to 1975. The difference in levels recorded is very substantial and is greatest toward the end of the series. No linear trends emerge in the non-urban or four-city data, and the trend in Dublin is curvilinear. The starkness of the contrast between Dublin and the other areas is duplicated in the detection rates shown in Table 13. In Dublin, only a small fraction of pedal cycle larcenies result in a suspect being identified, while in the four cities and in non-urban areas detection rates frequently exceeded 90 per cent. The detection rates in the latter two areas are essentially unchanged over the 12 years considered.

Table 11: *Larceny of motor vehicles per 10,000 registered vehicles*

Year	Area		
	Dublin	Four-cities	Non-Urban
1964	6.9	1.3	1.3
1965	7.6	1.3	0.7
1966	9.7	1.0	1.2
1967	13.8	1.7	2.2
1968	12.1	1.4	1.4
1969	23.9	0.8	1.6
1970	26.4	2.7	2.1
1971	43.3	5.9	5.3
1972	44.7	5.8	6.2
1973	29.2	1.3	6.6
1974	19.4	4.4	5.2
1975	28.2	2.7	4.8

Table 12: *Detection rates for larcenies of motor vehicles*

Year	Area		
	Dublin	Four-cities	Non-urban
	per cent	per cent	per cent
1964	35.8	62.5	93.3
1965	40.6	55.6	100.0
1966	31.0	42.9	94.1
1967	32.3	69.2	71.0
1968	25.2	72.7	90.5
1969	24.2	57.1	65.4
1970	23.4	32.0	62.1
1971	18.2	22.0	68.5
1972	19.6	27.4	61.5
1973	20.8	53.3	47.9
1974	24.0	17.3	50.0
1975	19.6	51.5	43.9

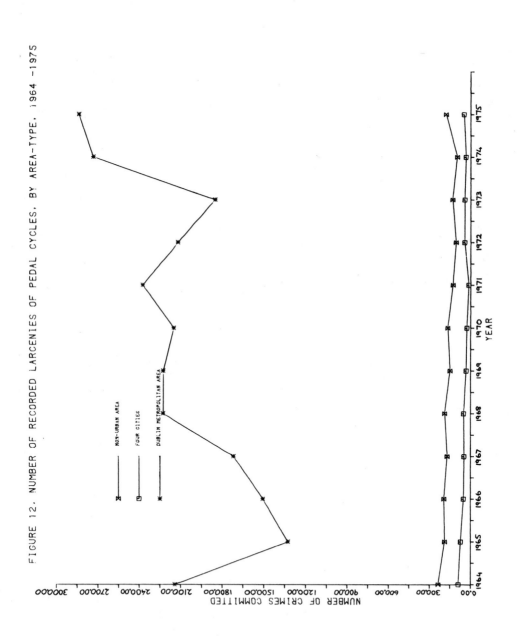

FIGURE 12. NUMBER OF RECORDED LARCENIES OF PEDAL CYCLES, BY AREA-TYPE, 1964 -1975

Table 13: *Detection rates for larcenies of pedal cycles*

	Area		
Year	*Dublin*	*Four-cities*	*Non-urban*
	per cent	*per cent*	*per cent*
1964	7.9	61.1	90.7
1965	13.7	63.0	96.8
1966	10.9	73.1	96.4
1967	12.8	73.5	94.2
1968	8.6	76.9	72.1
1969	6.2	76.5	98.7
1970	3.4	93.1	94.0
1971	2.4	93.8	90.8
1972	1.9	53.3	93.5
1973	2.6	56.8	88.0
1974	1.2	62.9	95.9
1975	1.1	91.8	57.9

Pedal cycle larceny is representative of property offences that tend to be less amenable to shifts in supply and less likely to be practised as an organised activity. That the potential for doing so is greater in a metropolitan centre such as Dublin may explain the discrepancy in trends present in Figure 12. But the magnitude of the discrepancy, and the absence of any upward trend outside of Dublin, reinforces the argument that the type of property interacts with other influences on changes in offence levels. There are, of course, difficulties in interpreting differences that emerge between types of offences. Unlike the other categories of property crime considered in this chapter, it can be assumed that pedal cycle larceny will tend to be committed by individuals living within the locality. It is therefore the category most susceptible to the differences between urban and non-urban law enforcement, though the similarity of trends in the four-cities and the non-urban areas suggests that other factors are operative.

The magnitude of the downward trend in the four-cities and in the non-urban areas is apparent when index numbers are examined. Taking the 1964 level of known offences as 100, the index numbers for Dublin, the four cities, and the non-urban areas are, respectively, 132.4, 54.5 and 75.8. Computing rates per 10,000 population for the 1975 levels similarly clarifies the differential between Dublin and other areas. There were 28.6 pedal cycle larcenies per 10,000 Dublin population; for the four cities and non-urban areas the comparable rates are 1.4 and 1.0.

Robbery·spans the boundaries between personal and property crime. It has a clear economic motivation, but involves confrontation: a robbery perforce includes an assault. Indeed, the ambiguity is such that robbery is perhaps the offence category most susceptible to classification error (Jacobson, 1975 p. 241). When urban/rural differences are studied using crime statistics drawn from a national police force, as in Ireland, the potential for that ambiguity to jeopardise the comparability of the trends is minimised. It is reasonable to assume that the same criteria are used in all areas to determine what comprises a robbery.

The trends by area shown in Figure 13 are all of substantial increase over the 12 years, though that for Dublin is the most striking. Despite the increases, it is useful to note the very low levels present in 1964, levels that are roughly equivalent in the three areas. When the 1964 totals are set to 100, the 1975 index numbers for Dublin, the four-cities, and the non-urban areas stand at 1,417.1, 875.0, and 726.3, respectively. As was the case for all the property offences considered, the highest levels are found in Dublin, followed by the non-urban areas. The rates per 10,000 population in 1975 were 5.0 in Dublin, 1.98 in the four-cities, and 0.76 in the non-urban areas. Despite the increase, robbery remains one of the least common property offences.

The robberies in the crime statistics vary from 10 pence taken by one child from another to a meticulously planned robbery of thousands of pounds. To the extent that the more careful the preparations and the more "rational" the target the lower the probability of detection, the detection rates in Table 14 provide some indication of the nature of the recorded robberies. Once again, there exists a clear and abrupt shift between two years in the detection rate. For Dublin, this shift is found in comparing the 1969 rate with the 1970 rate; for the four-cities and the non-urban areas, the relevant years are 1970 and 1971. As was the case for larceny from vehicles, the fall in the detection rate coincides with a sharp increase in incidence for both Dublin and the four-cities, but not for the non-urban areas. The most reasonable interpretation would allow for the pressures upon, and changes within, the gardai, over those years, though some of the decline doubtlessly reflects changes in the frequency and the nature of the robberies occurring.

The use of a real or imitation firearm in the course of a robbery – whether successful or attempted – results in the entry of an offence into the subcategory of armed robbery. Two such entries were recorded in 1964. Twelve years later, the number recorded had risen to 153. Those 153 offences, representing 21.7 per cent of all recorded robberies in the year 1975, were apportioned such that 53.6 per cent were in Dublin, 9.2 per cent in the four-

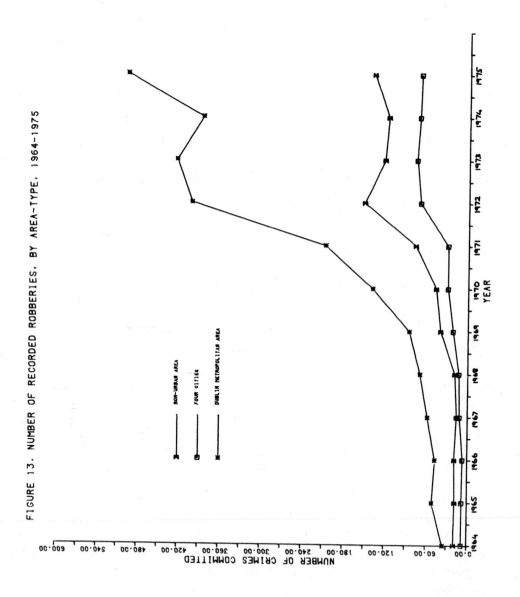

FIGURE 13. NUMBER OF RECORDED ROBBERIES, BY AREA-TYPE, 1964-1975

cities, and 37.3 per cent in the non-urban areas. That distribution is roughly equivalent to that obtaining for 1973 and 1974. The 1964–1975 levels of known armed robberies by area-types are given in Table 15.

Table 14: *Detection rates for robberies*

	Dublin	Four-cities	Non-urban
	per cent	per cent	per cent
1964	74.3	100.0	100.0
1965	74.5	75.0	77.8
1966	87.2	85.7	73.7
1967	70.7	83.3	87.5
1968	75.4	84.6	73.7
1969	72.9	86.4	90.0
1970	57.2	73.3	80.9
1971	49.3	56.7	39.0
1972	51.1	60.0	33.8
1973	56.0	64.5	53.3
1974	47.3	58.3	51.3
1975	42.7	61.4	46.4

Table 15: *Incidence of armed robberies: 1964–1975**

Year	Dublin	Four-cities	Non-urban	National
1964	2	0	0	2
1965	2	1	0	3
1966	1	1	0	2
1967	3	0	0	3
1968	2	0	1	3
1969	6	2	4	12
1970	12	1	4	17
1971	10	1	19	30
1972	57	7	68	132
1973	68	10	45	123
1974	72	5	50	127
1975	82	14	57	153

*An armed robbery is one in which a firearm – real or imitation – is alleged to have been used.

Burglary, larceny from motor vehicles, robbery, and like offences, all have a potential for being conducted on a rational, organised basis, but embrace a wide range of behaviour. The incidence of the offence of receiving stolen property is perhaps the most direct measure of the extent to which crime is pursued as a business enterprise. For a market in illicitly obtained goods to flourish, middlemen linking suppliers with purchasers are a prerequisite. The trends in Figure 14 are therefore of considerable interest. While the number of known receiving offences remains low for Dublin, but not for the other area-types, the trend in increase is clear. In the non-urban areas, the increase is erratic, and is ultimately reversed. This is the only offence in which the hierarchical ranking of incidence by area fails to remain consistent across the 12 years, with the levels in non-urban areas often exceeding those in Dublin. The 1975 index numbers are 365.0 in Dublin, 104.3 in the four-cities, and 122.2 in the non-urban areas.

The detection rates here cannot illuminate differences between the three areas. Nowhere during the 12 years does that rate fall below 97.4 per cent. Receiving offences can only become "known" during the course of a garda investigation; where gardai are aware of the existence of such an offence they will almost inevitably be aware of the individual they consider responsible.

When rates are calculated per 10,000 population in each type of area, the ordering among the areas changes. In 1975 the incidence of receiving offences per 10,000 population was 2.2 in Dublin, 2.06 in the four-cities, and 1.0 in the non-urban areas.

Where other property offences registered three-fold and greater increases over the 12 years, the number of known receiving offences remained essentially unchanged. Moreover, receiving offences were less prone than other property offences to be concentrated in Dublin. This suggests a lack of sophistication in the execution and exploitation of property offences generally, and, less firmly, that the bulk of the increase in recorded property offences can be attributed to new recruits entering this area of enterprise rather than to an increased efficiency on the part of long-standing practitioners. If conclusions here are particularly elusive, it is because the total of known receiving offences for any given year is highly sensitive to the amount of resources devoted to special investigations during the year.

Offences Against Persons

The status of offences against persons, such as assault, is uncertain within both the social disorganisation and the structural perspectives. Both perspectives are intended primarily as explanations of changes in property crime. Therefore, the inclusion of person offences is often merely as a point of comparison to the property crimes that form the major interest. Where an ex-

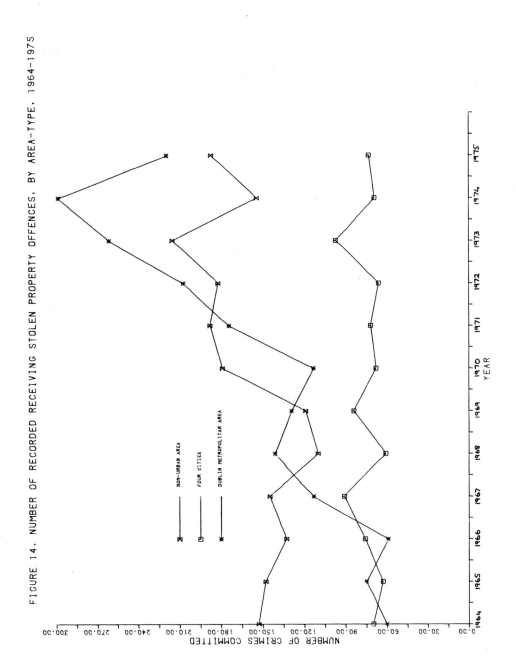

FIGURE 14. NUMBER OF RECORDED RECEIVING STOLEN PROPERTY OFFENCES, BY AREA-TYPE, 1964–1975

planation for the level of assault or homicide is attempted, the standard treatment is to argue that such offences are influenced by normative considerations. A subculture of violence is identified – specific to groups defined by some combination of regional location, ethnicity, and age – in which the dominant values and beliefs, in contrast to those found in the population at large, encourage and facilitate violence. As described by Wolfgang and Ferracuti (1967), the members of such groups are disproportionately the victims and the perpetrators of homicides and assaults. The over-representation of young men from particular minority groups is therefore to be explained by their adherence to a normative system that rejects the conventional inhibitions on resorting to violence. The use of violence is instead considered honourable, and indeed it many situations, a required response to the actions of others.

If this argument is adopted, there is no clear basis for anticipating urban/rural differences in offences against persons, or for predicting the trends that will accompany social change. However, Jacobson (1975) provides a point of reference through the results of his comparison of crime rates in southern and non-southern American cities: a convergence between the regions began with changes in the property crime rate, followed after an interval by changes in the rate of crimes against persons. This lag was interpreted as the result of industrialisation and urbanisation first creating socio-economic and demographic change that ultimately generated the normative transformation to which violent crimes responded.

The national trend in assault, shown in Chapter 4, did indeed depart substantially from trends in property crime. An upward trend in the level of indictable assault began in the 1950s and continued unabated over the 25 years, forming a gradual growth curve. The structural break, so evident for other offences, was nowhere present in the case of assault. Thus, it can be concluded that if social structural change is influencing the trend in offences against persons, it is doing so in a manner that differs significantly from what occurred for property offences. The possibility of establishing a link between structural change and person offences will be the topic of a separate chapter – Chapter 6 – and for the present the trends in assault will be used as a counterweight to those found for property offences.

The extent to which urban/non-urban differences in levels of assault existed and persist in Ireland can be gauged from Figure 15. The number of known indictable assaults is consistently highest in the non-urban areas throughout the 12 years, the next highest levels being found in Dublin. An overall linear trend is present for all three area-types, though the increase is not continuous, and the patterns vary considerably among the areas. For Dublin, when the offences known in 1964 are set equal to 100, the index for

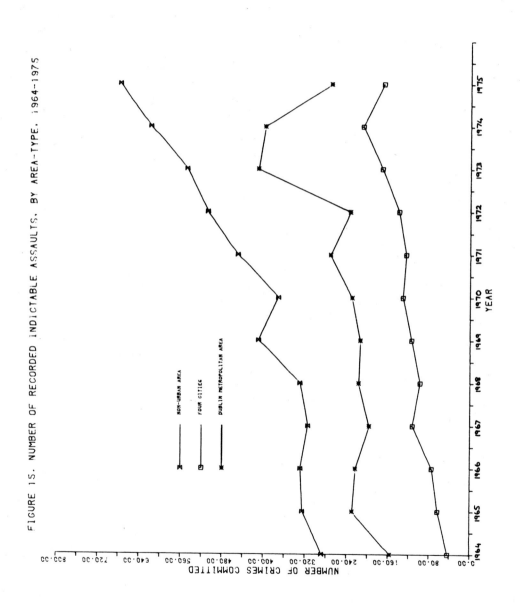

FIGURE 15. NUMBER OF RECORDED INDICTABLE ASSAULTS, BY AREA-TYPE, 1964-1975

1975 stands at 173.7. The 1975 index numbers for the four-cities and the non-urban areas are 395.3 and 235.4 respectively. The clearest difference between the areas is that while in Dublin and the four-cities the number of assaults was stable during the last six years, assaults in the non-urban areas evinced an almost precisely linear increase.

The use of crime rates reflecting the population at risk is perhaps most meaningful when examining assault statistics. For 1975, the rates so derived for Dublin, the four-cities, and non-urban areas are, respectively, 2.7, 4.8 and 3.7. This does not conform to the order among area-types found for property offences, and does not replicate the pattern of other countries in which violent crime is often a strongly non-urban phenomenon. Further, the pattern of convergence of regional crime rates identified by Jacobson (1975) was not replicated in the data for Ireland. Trends for assaults were distributed among the regions in much the same manner as were those for property offences. The only major difference present reverses the pattern found in the United States: in the Irish data the largest increases in assaults occurred in the initial years of the time-period for urban areas, while those for property offences were concentrated somewhat later.

When the detection rates in Table 16 are examined, a clear divergence is evident between Dublin and the other areas. For the four-cities and non-urban areas, no trend is discernible; the detection rates throughout approach 100 per cent. The rates for Dublin, while still high, are consistently and substantially lower. Given that the higher the detection rate for such offences, the greater the likelihood that the participants in the assaults knew one another, a qualitative, as well as quantitative, difference appears to exist between the areas. When adjusted for population, the four-cities have a high rate of incidence and a high rate of detection; in contrast, the non-urban areas have a moderate level of incidence and a high rate of detection, and Dublin a low level of incidence and a comparatively low detection rate.

What most clearly differentiates assaults in the Dublin Metropolitan Area from those occurring elsewhere is the proportion in which gardai are the victims. In 1975, gardai were the victims in 8.5 per cent of all assaults in Dublin, 32.5 per cent in the four-cities, and 41.5 per cent in the non-urban areas. For 1972, the earliest year for which comparable data are available, 10.7 per cent of Dublin assaults had gardai as the victims; this was true in 32.9 per cent of assaults in the four-cities, and 39.7 per cent of non-urban assaults. Therefore, though the bulk of assaults consistently occurs outside of Dublin, if only assaults on "civilians" are used as the basis for comparison, the differences narrow substantially.

How reliable is the number of known assaults as an indicator of the extent of interpersonal violence? That even in Dublin 75 per cent of all assaults were detected in 1975 suggests that randomly directed violence is infrequent. While this speaks to the nature of assaults in Ireland, and to the difference in that regard between Dublin and the rest of the country, it may still be the case that police intervention occurs only in the most serious assaults. McClintock (1963) argues that the number of recorded assaults is very sensitive to changing public and police tolerance of violence. This suggests both the possibility of a substantial quantity of unrecorded assaults – the ominously named "dark figure" of crime – and that a linear trend of increasing assault statistics partly reflects changing attitudes, with a growing intolerance of violence leading to an increasing proportion of assaults becoming "known". It is unlikely, however, that the trends in Figure 15 merely outline the iceberg's tip. A high level of interpersonal violence implies a substantial homicide rate (see Walker, 1968 p. 21; Zimring 1972). The correlation between annual levels of known homicides and known indictable assaults in Ireland for the 1964 to 1975 period is 0.86 reflecting the common upward trend in the two series. Thus, though indictable assault covers a wide range of interpersonal violence – roughly all those inflicting or intending clear physical or mental harm – it does seem a reasonable indicator for this study.

Table 16: *Detection rates for indictable assaults*

Year	Dublin	Four-cities	Non-urban
	per cent	per cent	per cent
1964	88.5	100.0	99.3
1965	93.4	100.0	98.5
1966	86.1	100.0	99.7
1967	88.8	99.1	98.4
1968	88.9	95.9	98.5
1969	87.9	100.0	98.3
1970	85.2	97.7	97.6
1971	83.1	98.4	97.6
1972	80.9	96.4	92.3
1973	84.2	98.3	98.2
1974	78.1	98.1	97.9
1975	74.9	98.8	97.1

A Comparison of Trends in Known Offences

Thus far, the assessment of urban/rural differences in trends has relied on inspection of tables and figures. The sheer number of trend lines, percentages, and rates has overburdened what is at best an imprecise mode of analysis. This section uses correlations to formalise the comparisons. First, the inter-correlations among offence categories are examined separately for each type of area. The correlation coefficients will indicate the extent to which a type of area has a clear pattern of change, common to all offence categories, and the extent to which those patterns are distinctive to Dublin, the four-cities, and non-urban areas. A second table of correlations measures the strength of relationship between the trends in the three types of areas, examining each offence category separately.

The most appropriate mathematical representation of the trends in known offences found in the preceding figures is one of growth by a constant absolute change per unit of time – a standard linear trend. Perhaps because of the limited time span, this basic form appears to characterise the trends for all offence categories and all types of areas. However, it remains possible to question the degree of covariation that is present among the series. A common linear trend over the 12 years assures high correlations, but it is equally important to establish whether there is also a common pattern of movement around the trend lines. For example, in those years in which housebreaking exceeds the level anticipated on the basis of the linear trend, is the same true of shopbreaking or of assault? To obtain answers to such questions it is necessary to employ variables that have been de-trended.

De-trending is accomplished here, as in Chapter 4, by obtaining the correlations among residuals, the residuals being derived by regressing each offence category on time. The coefficients in Table 17 provide the intercorrelations among nine indicators used in the two previous sections. Coefficients above the diagonal in each matrix are the standard zero-order correlations, calculated on the basis of the number of known offences. The contrasting set of coefficients among residuals, representing the relationships after de-trending, are found in the lower triangle.

Table 17 is useful because it summarises the extent to which indicators in each area-type are acting consistently. Generally speaking, there is a strong consistency in the non-urban areas, moderate consistency in Dublin, and little evident consistency in the four-cities. This difference is clearest in the case of the offence level property crime indicators. In the non-urban areas, if pedal cycle larceny is excluded, the intercorrelations are substantial, even when the relationships have been de-trended. This is also true for Dublin, though the relationships are less substantial. The correlations present among those indicators in the four-cities, however, are weak. For example, though larceny

Table 17: *Intercorrelations among offence indicators, 1964–1975**

Dublin metropolitan area

	1.	2.	3.	4.	5.	6.	7.	8.	9.
1. Assault	1.0	.71	.52	.53	.72	.86	.44	.30	.31
2. Housebreaking	-.13	1.0	.94	.94	.95	.89	.82	.70	.65
3. Shopbreaking	-.76	.25	1.0	.89	.85	.76	.71	.80	.70
4. Larceny from vehicles	-.50	.64	.25	1.0	.88	.77	.94	.67	.65
5. Robbery	.15	.57	-.14	.24	1.0	.89	.76	.58	.44
6. Receiving	.69	-.31	-.74	-.41	.28	1.0	.67	.62	.46
7. Larceny of vehicles	-.34	.40	-.16	.85	.13	-.22	1.0	.48	.58
8. Pedal cycle larceny	-.45	.06	.56	.08	-.26	-.09	-.18	1.0	.53
9. Property value	-.36	-.17	.28	.12	-.67	-.53	.10	.10	1.0

Four-cities

	1.	2.	3.	4.	5.	6.	7.	8.	9.
1. Assault	1.0	.88	.82	.81	.89	.24	.60	-.64	-.38
2. Housebreaking	-.32	1.0	.94	.96	.88	.15	.54	-.47	.00
3. Shopbreaking	-.54	.51	1.0	.94	.82	-.01	.68	-.55	-.03
4. Larceny from vehicles	-.48	.77	.57	1.0	.90	.07	.60	-.33	.08
5. Robbery	.08	.03	-.31	.39	1.0	.17	.63	-.38	-.12
6. Receiving	.34	.05	-.38	-.16	.10	1.0	-.28	-.18	-.36
7. Larceny of vehicles	-.15	-.44	.22	-.03	.05	-.51	1.0	-.55	-.18
8. Pedal cycle larceny	-.16	.58	.13	.81	.70	-.12	-.22	1.0	.58
9. Property value	-.67	.63	.40	.64	.15	-.35	-.07	.60	1.0

Non-urban areas

	1.	2.	3.	4.	5.	6.	7.	8.	9.
1. Assault	1.0	.96	.93	.97	.92	.58	.89	-.77	.88
2. Housebreaking	.68	1.0	.95	.97	.89	.63	.85	-.67	.85
3. Shopbreaking	.36	.64	1.0	.98	.94	.78	.93	-.75	.89
4. Larceny from vehicles	.62	.79	.82	1.0	.94	.67	.91	-.81	.91
5. Robbery	.48	.36	.63	.66	1.0	.71	.95	-.80	.82
6. Receiving	.05	.25	.84	.51	.49	1.0	.77	-.46	.60
7. Larceny of vehicles	.27	.12	.60	.36	.75	.67	1.0	-.82	.79
8. Pedal cycle larceny	.19	.54	.29	.20	-.18	.10	-.27	1.0	-.68
9. Property value	-.05	-.08	.06	-.06	-.12	.16	-.28	.56	1.0

*Coefficients above the diagonal in each matrix are zero-order correlations based on the level of known offences; coefficients below the diagonal in each matrix are zero-order correlations based on the residuals derived from regressing each offence variable against time.

from vehicles has a correlation of .94 with the level of larceny of vehicles in Dublin and .91 in the non-urban areas, the correlation in the four-cities data is .60. Similarly, the correlations linking larceny of vehicles to receiving offences are .67 and .77 in Dublin and the non-urban areas, respectively, and −.28 in the four-cities.

Larceny of pedal cycles and the average value of property stolen in burglaries are the anomalies to the basic consistency present in Table 17 among the property crime indicators. Pedal cycle larceny levels, with the exception of the consistently negative relationships found in the non-urban areas, are not systematically related to other property crimes. For the average value of stolen property, again with the exception of the non-urban areas, the correlations with the levels of burglary are insubstantial. So again it is the cohesiveness of the indicators outside of the cities that is most interesting.

The use of correlations based on residuals essentially reinforces what the relationships based on levels indicated. Overall, those correlations are weak or negative in Dublin and in the four-cities, and comparatively stronger in the non-urban areas. This occurs despite the diversity of the areas subsumed in the latter category. The trends for the non-urban parts of the country are consistent for all the offence categories, though the de-trended relationships of property offences to the average value of stolen property are negligible. With that exception, the indicators share both a common linear trend and a common pattern of movement around that trend.

The reverse of that finding can describe the relationships among the indicators in the four-cities. Perhaps because of differences among the cities, no pattern emerges. The indicators appear to be moving without reference to each other.

The three indicators for burglary – housebreaking, shopbreaking, and property value – are less strongly correlated once the upward linear trend is removed. Housebreaking and shopbreaking have residual correlations of .25 in Dublin, .51 in the four-cities, and .64 in non-urban areas. Small or negative correlations associate those offences with property value in Dublin and the non-urban areas, while moderately positive relationships occur in the four-cities. The significance of the four-cities relationships, however, can be overstated – the linear trend in that area for average value of stolen property is slight and deviations from that trend do not have the importance of those found in the other two areas.

The examination of correlations based on residuals reinforces the distinctiveness of the non-urban areas previously found using standard correlations. It also suggests that in urban areas the offence categories respond to economic or social conditions in a manner less monolithic than might be judged from the charts used previously; fluctuations around the trend line differ considerably among the offences. In Dublin, for example, the zero-order relationship between receiving stolen goods and shopbreaking is .76, but the correlation with the linear component removed is –.74. The use of correlations among residuals imposes a more stringent test for the presence and strength of a relationship.

Table 18 provides a further basis for comparing the three types of areas. The correlations between areas are given separately for each offence category, again adopting the convention of contrasting correlations derived from levels of known offences with those based on residuals.

When the recorded offence level is used, the coefficients reinforce the impression of a high degree of consistency among major property crimes: housebreaking, shopbreaking, and robbery. For those offences, correlations of .90 or greater link the three types of areas. The indicators of the level of sophistication in property crime – receiving stolen property and average value of stolen property – show a different pattern, with correlations of .73 and .53, respectively, relating Dublin and the non-urban areas, and slight or negative correlations relating the four-cities to other areas. Overall, trends in Dublin and non-urban areas evince the greatest similarity, though there does appear to be a pattern of movement in levels of known offences that is national rather than peculiar to types of areas. Both that pattern and the close connection between Dublin and non-urban trends are reflected in the correlations based on residuals. Consistency across areas is most evident for the offence of robbery: even after de-trending, correlations between areas exceed .83 (the correlations based on numbers of offences exceeded .97). Generally, the highest correlations are for the major forms of property crime and the weakest relationships are for the minor property offences of larceny from vehicles and pedal cycle larceny. The correlations linking the two urban areas are not systematically stronger than urban/non-urban relationships. For average values of stolen property, the highest correlation is the .37 between Dublin and the non-urban areas. The other measure of sophistication used for property crime, receiving stolen property, does not provide evidence of common movement around the trends. Assaults, whether correlated through levels or residuals, do not have the consistency across areas found for most property crimes.

The correlations found in Tables 17 and 18 complement the conclusions drawn earlier in the chapter from the inspection of figures and tables. Trends over the 12 years act to homogenise far more than to differentiate areas. The more dependent an offence category is on a specific form of property, the stronger the relationship between areas proves to be, and often the most forceful the link is between Dublin and the non-urban areas. It is in those two areas that property crime can be seen to become both more prevalent and

Table 18: *Correlations among area offence levels: 1964–1975*

	Offence levels			Residuals		
	Dublin/ four-cities	*Dublin/ non-urban*	*Four-cities/ non-urban*	*Dublin/ four-cities*	*Dublin/ non-urban*	*Four-cities/ non-urban*
Assault	.82	.74	.88	.56	.20	−.13
Housebreaking	.97	.95	.97	.48	.67	.74
Shopbreaking	.99	.90	.92	.93	.11	.34
Larceny from vehicles	.87	.94	.96	.24	.60	.76
Robbery	.98	.98	.97	.86	.88	.83
Receiving	.18	.53	.27	.13	−.07	.23
Larceny of vehicles	.81	.84	.72	.62	.49	.38
Pedal cycles	−.39	−.45	.73	.10	.38	.47
Property value	−.29	.73	−.14	−.23	.37	.10

more successfully practised as an organised and profitable enterprise.

Conclusion

The 1964 to 1975 trends for the nine crime indicators have been examined separately for three types of areas selected to approximate urban/rural differences. Though the contribution made by increases in the urban areas, and particularly in Dublin, to the national level trends discussed in Chapter 4 was clearly greater than that made by changes in the non-urban areas, the differential is not dramatic. The predominance of urban trends in shaping the upward movement in the crime statistics is obvious only for housebreaking, and larceny from vehicles. In all other instances, the non-urban areas recorded increases equivalent to those in the two urban areas or in excess of those found in the four-cities. And in one indicator, the average value of property stolen in burglaries, the increase in non-urban areas is nearly twice as great as that in Dublin and more than three times as great as that in the four-cities.

Overall, therefore, the evidence assembled in this chapter argues for the essential similarity across types of areas. Urban and rural differences do exist, and did become somewhat accentuated over the 12 years, but the upward pattern is clear in all areas. Moreover, the sequencing of large increments over that period is quite similar.

The possible influence of differences in police procedures and activities in urban and non-urban areas on the trends was considered. Though detection rates for several offence categories were substantially lower in Dublin than elsewhere, such differences do not appear to threaten the meaningfulness of comparing the trends for the three types of areas. Further, the abrupt shift at the start of the new decade to lower detection levels was apparently a truly national phenomenon. While that shift cannot be fully explained, its presence in all three areas largely precludes any distortion of the changes recorded in offence levels that could affect the comparisons I made.

If the evidence presented in this chapter on the extent of urban and rural differences in the 1964–75 trends is apportioned between the two perspectives, the weight added to the structural perspective is the more substantial. The increases in crime levels were, by and large, reflected everywhere. There was no consistency among the eight property crime indicators in which area recorded the greatest increase. Dublin was the location for the greatest increases in shopbreaking, larceny of motor vehicles, pedal cycle larceny, robbery, and receiving stolen property. The four-cities had the most substantial increases in housebreaking and larceny from vehicles, while the average value of stolen property changed most dramatically in the non-urban areas. Both the charts and the statistical analysis indicated that the Dublin trends often shared more characteristics with those in the non-urban areas than with what occurred in the four-cities.

The trends for indictable assault do not produce a clearer differentiation among the areas. In Dublin and the non-urban areas, the level of assault was about two times greater in 1975; the increase in the four-cities was about four-fold. The sequencing of those increases, however, does differ between urban and non-urban areas, with the non-urban increases concentrated in the last six years of the period and those in the urban areas evenly distributed. As in the national trends, the urban/rural comparisons suggest that property crime and person offences are responding to rather different influences. This emerged quite clearly in the correlational analysis.

As a social problem, increasing crime rates cannot be isolated as urban-based or even as Dublin-based. The consistency in trends, whether gauged from charts or from correlations, is impressive, particularly for the major forms of property crime, such as burglary and motor vehicle larceny. Problems of law enforcement also do not appear to be markedly greater in urban contexts. If the percentage of detections achieved is used to measure success, then for most offences gardai outside of urban areas do not appear to be at an advantage. Such differences as do exist, in which Dublin gardai appear at a disadvantage compared to their counterparts elsewhere, generally have been diminishing since the mid-1960s. This has occurred through a general lowering of the detection rate. However, it should be stressed that for most offences it is a rate which remains quite high. The changes reflected in the trends for detection rates, like those for offence levels, stress the common experience since the mid-1960s in all areas, not the differences.

The stability over the 12 years in the distribution of known offences suggests, but does not establish, that the geographical impact of economic and social change on crime statistics in Ireland was diffuse rather than concentrated in cities. In other Western countries, crime statistics tended to increase gradually through a lengthy series of annual increases and with a clear sequence of first registering an impact in urban areas, an impact that was felt considerably later in rural areas. The magnitude of the increases in Ireland between 1964 and 1975 may be explicable on this basis. A transformation in the extent and nature of officially recorded crime that in the United States and in much of Europe was accomplished by gradual accretion, was in Ireland crowded into little more than a decade. It was a transformation not by stages but by one rapid step.

Chapter 6

Homicide and Social Change

Introduction

This chapter adapts the data on homicide, by far the most detailed and accurate information available on crime in Ireland, to serve several purposes.
First, since garda statistics on the number of homicides that occurred in particular years and in particular areas are not susceptible to major problems of
under-reporting, it will be possible to measure more precisely than previously
the changes that have occurred in the level and location of violent crimes
against persons. Precision is further enhanced by the detail of the information
available on homicide: a full transformation of the homicide statistics into a
consistent series is possible. Such adjustments are not possible for other offences, and as will be seen, the resulting changes in annual figures are substantial. Second, the wealth of information on the participants in, and the circumstances of, homicide incidents allows me to express the impact of social
change in terms of specific types of people and relationships. Hitherto the
analysis has been depersonalised, examining changes in aggregate statistics.
For homicide, it is possible to portray crime as an aspect of human behaviour.

This ability to move beyond aggregate levels and to cast off the restraints
imposed by the classifications and definitions used in producing the *Report on
Crime* derives from access to the complete files for all homicides recorded in
the 1950s and the 1970s. It was, therefore, possible to reconstruct the incident
itself and to select the information to be used for its description.

That freedom to reconstruct events has made police homicide files a major
resource for social historians. Violent death – in nineteenth-century
Philadelphia (Lane, 1979) or in Paris under the Directory (Cobb, 1978) – has
been used as a window on a particular era, a portrait of a social order. As
Lane (1979, p. 1) expresses the possibilities:

> . . . the real subject is life, the living behaviour of thousands of
> largely anonymous Philadelphians . . . Of many of these people, the
> only record that remains is the final entry: perhaps a story in the
> paper, more surely a brief notation by some agent of the state of in-
> formation incident to the way in which they died. The manner of
> dying is, however, often a reflection of the manner of living, and
> these largely unexplored records may provide much new informa-
> tion about the changing conditions of ordinary life.

The use to be made of homicide data here is more modest. Characteristics of
individuals, both victims and offenders, will be used to link the social struc-

tural changes outlined in Chapter 2 with the distribution of interpersonal violence.

Though homicide is not being used in this study as a metaphor for a particular social structure, a claim is made that the level and the distribution of homicide reflects those of violent assaultive crimes generally. It has been shown in other countries that the demarcation between murder and assault is highly fluid: motivation, intention, and action do not differ substantially in most fatal incidents from those in which less serious injuries are inflicted (Walker, 1968, p. 21; Zimring, 1972). A homicide is often an assault that succeeds. Where violence is widespread, a proportion of all incidents will result in a death, and, therefore, in the recording of a murder or manslaughter in the official crime statistics. The pattern of homicide in Ireland during the periods of interest can be treated as a surrogate for interpersonal violence.

The first section of this chapter describes the data that have been collected on homicide and the resulting trends in offence levels for the 1951 to 1975 period. In the second section, I return to some unfinished business from Chapter 2: the development of an explanation of changes in levels and patterns of crimes against persons that builds on the basic premise of the structural perspective. It is argued that the most important link between structural change and interpersonal violence is the changes that occur in mechanisms for conflict regulation. Various positions within a social structure – as defined by occupations, regions, and age – can be anticipated to be conducive to violence. Such positions have a potential for conflict in particular relationships together with a set of resources and mechanisms to cope with it. That perspective is applied in the third section of the chapter to conditions in Ireland during the 1950s and 1970s, and the resulting expectations as to the extent and nature of homicide are tested in the fourth section. In doing so, the focus is on changes in the nature of homicide, particularly as expressed in the age differences between victim and offender. The typology of homicide used ranges from *inter*-generational to *intra*-generational.

Data on Homicide

On the first consideration, homicide seems a particularly tractable form of crime, the finality of the victim's death lending it to a definition absent from other offence categories. This is not entirely true. The boundaries of the legal offence of homicide are made ambiguous by the necessity of excluding instances in which death was the result of negligence, and of making distinctions in terms of intention and motivation.

Traffic fatalities are thus excluded from the homicide data, except in the rare instance in which a motor vehicle is used deliberately as an instrument of death, as the person responsible lacks culpability. A special category, infanticide, was established under the Infanticide Act of 1949, in which the effects of childbirth are assumed to mitigate in those instances in which a mother is responsible for the death of a child less than one year old. It is excluded. This leaves two basic categories of homicide on which this chapter will focus: murder and manslaughter. Murder is killing with malice aforethought, with a clear intention to harm. Where that intention was absent, or where provocation existed, the lesser offence of manslaughter can be used. The distinction between murder and manslaughter is not an important one for the purposes of this study, though obviously it is of considerable moment to a defendant. The classification of manslaughter can only be used if a suspect has been identified, and the decision as to the offence in which a prosecution will be undertaken does not necessarily reflect differences among incidents that would be of interest here.

Murders and manslaughters in which the victims are more than one year old form the operational definition of homicide used here. Victims of car bomb explosions, of whom there were five in 1973 and 33 in 1974, are excluded as their deaths are unlikely to prove revealing of the nature of homicide within the intentions of this study. Victims of political assassinations or sectarian killings are included. In any case, it would be impossible to exclude them with certainty. Therefore, homicide constitutes all killings of designated victims more than one year old. It is the death that creates the discontinuity between homicides and other assaults: "most violent attacks with deadly weapons, whether fatal or non-fatal, are pursued with ambiguous intentions as to whether the victim should die" (Zimring, 1972, p. 111).

Table 19 provides the numbers of homicides so defined that occurred in each year between 1951 and 1975. The numbers are adjusted to reflect the most up-to-date information available, which results in some instances to offences listed in the *Report on Crime* as murder being treated here as manslaughter. All figures refer to calendar years. The most important adjustment, however, is to standardise the unit of counting. The *Report on Crime* in the years of interest has used two methods of counting the number of homicides. In some years, the total is that of *incidents*, with one incident possibly subsuming several deaths; an alternative counting procedure is to enter a homicide for each death, there being as many homicides as there were victims. It should also be noted that the numbers cited in Table 19 are instances in which a homicide has officially been noted. The acquittal of a particular defendant does not alter that classification.

The trend over the 25 years towards an increasing level of homicide is clear, but it occurs erratically. That is perhaps inevitable given the small numbers involved. When the change is expressed as averages, however, the upward tendency becomes clear. In the 1950s, the average number of annual homicides was 7.2, in the 1960s, 10.1, and for the six years 1970–75, 20.8.

The remainder of this chapter is devoted to a study of the homicides from two distinct periods: (1) the ten years, 1951–60, and (2) the five years, 1970–74. A description will be given before the data analysis of the variables that have been abstracted from the files on homicide.

Table 19. *Incidence of homicide and infanticide 1951–1975*
Calendar Years

Year	(1) Murder	(2) Manslaughter	(3) Homicide (1) + (2)	(4) Infanticide[1]
1951	02	03	05	03
1952	03	03	06	07
1953	08	07	15	05*
1954	02	01	03	02
1955	05	02	07	04
1956	03	03	06	01
1957	06	02	08	06
1958	07	00	07	04
1959	07	01	08	02
1960	00	02	02	02
1961	09	04	13	03
1962	03	04	07	04
1963	05	02	07	01
1964	04	04	08	02
1965	09	07	16	01
1966	05	06	11	02
1967	09	03	12	01
1968	07	03	10	02
1969	09	06	15	01
1970	06	09	15	02
1971	12	07	19	02
1972	11	10	21	03
1973	18	08	26**	02
1974	09	11	20***	00
1975	20	04	24	00

[1]Includes all murder and manslaughter victims aged one year and under.
*Excludes 5 victims of infanticide discovered in 1953 and treated in the *Report on Crime* as one offence, the actual dates of death being unknown.
**Excludes 5 victims of car bomb explosions.
***Excludes 33 victims of car bomb explosions.

Homicide and Social Structure

The use of the concept of stress to mediate the impact of societal conditions on the potential for violence of particular individuals or groups defines the basic model for a structural approach to the study of violence. Within this approach, two ways of specifying the structure—stress—violence connection can be identified. Both depend on the premise that a social structure has an associated distribution of stress and coping resources among the extant demographic and class groupings.

In the first, and more familiar, formulation, stress is translated into subjective experience through a process by which individuals assess their "objective" conditions as constituting a state of "relative deprivation" (Henry and Short, 1954; Wood, 1961; Coser, 1970). This line of argument is most convincingly deployed in Wood's (1961) study of homicide in post-colonial Ceylon in which structural locations esteemed within the traditional ascribed status system of caste, but *disreputable* within the now ascendant achieved status system, are singled out as conducive to homicide.

The second view, within which stress is a potential property of certain roles or relationships, focuses on the social links of killers to victims (Bohannan, 1960; Goode, 1973). In Bohannan's (1960) study of African homicide, a pattern of homicide reveals "points of stress" within a society; a homicide "indicates the anomic state of the institution with which it is connected" (1960, p. 235). He argues from an assessment of the state of the major institutional orders that particular relationships are especially stress-laden. Because of the nature of the institutions in which they are located, participants in those relationships are most "at risk" as victims or as killers. The stress that is the motivating force in this formulation has its ultimate reference at an individual level, but Bohannan's explanatory framework is at the structural level: structural factors increase or diminish the propensity to violence in a relationship. This approach to the study of homicide, a fusion of a Durkheimian perspective on deviance with an anthropologist's ethnographic research tradition, offers a more appropriate base for the sociological study of violence than "relative deprivation" theory.

Goode's (1973) essay on violence among intimates contains a more coherent theoretical specification of the structural antecedents to violence in relationships. It allows us to replace Bohannan's emphasis on the vague concept of stress with a focus on the efficacy of institutionalised methods for coping with stress. Variation among structural locations in the possibilities for avoiding and resolving disputes is given particular emphasis (Goode, 1973, pp. 184–187). Structural locations differ in the ranges of satisfactions and pleasures that are available, as well as in the availability of non-violent techniques for conflict resolution. In the African tribes Bohannan studied, a category of social relationships could be abstracted for study, and its propensity to stress considered; in an industrial society the potential for violence is not intrinsic to a type of relationship but rather assumes a value determined by the structural locations of the participants. At each structural location the intensity of conflict among the participants in a type of relationship, together with the mitigating influence of the available coping resources, yields the potential for violence associated with that type of relationship.

Where mutually understood rules and symbols contain hostilities, threats and even blows may be exchanged without necessarily endangering the survival of the parties to a conflict or of their relationship. It is when the level of stress within a relationship exceeds the capacity of institutionalised coping procedures that injury and death become real potentials. To the extent that conflict is successfully institutionalised, clearly defined "termination points" to episodes of conflict, or to series of such episodes, are operative (Coser, 1970, pp. 37–51). Therefore, to adopt Goode's approach is not to equate conflict with pathology. As Simmel (1923/1955, p. 17) observed: "A certain amount of discord, inner divergence and outer controversy, is organically tied up with the very elements that ultimately hold the group together; it cannot be separated from the unity of the sociological structure". As a static theory, the argument treating violence as a property of types of relationship can be summarised as follows: structural inequalities are concomitant with a distribution of conflict potential and conflict regulation mechanisms that shape the pattern of homicide at particular structural locations. At any structural location, relationships where conflict cannot be institutionally regulated will be over-represented in the incidence of homicide. That over-representation should give each structural location a distinctive pattern of age differences between victims and offenders, with homicides varying on a dimension of inter-generational to intra-generational.

To employ this formulation in the study of change requires identification of those locations and relationships experiencing the most substantial alteration in levels of conflict and in modes of conflict regulation. First, the pervasive structural changes of the period in question must be delineated; then it is possible to assess the implications of change for basic categories of relationship in terms of the ability to control conflict. Though only the rudiments of a theory, this provides a procedure for studying homicide in periods of social change. By applying that procedure to Ireland during the last quarter century, a preliminary assessment of its efficacy can be made.

A Perspective on Irish Homicide

Two periods, the 1950s and the 1970s, have been singled out for study. These can be described as periods of secondary social change in Ireland during which institutions and roles adjusted to major disjunctures in social structure. The impact of structural change in each period can be construed in terms of differences established between urban and rural areas, between occupational categories, and between regions. An assessment of the effects of structural change on conflict potential and conflict regulation will be made for three broad categories of relationship – family, acquaintance, and stranger – which will be further differentiated in the course of the exposition.

During the 1940s a rapid decline in agricultural employment, without a compensating expansion in service or industrial employment, ensured that the consequences of structural change during the 1950s were more acute in rural than in urban areas. It was the small farmers of Connacht and West Munster – the western region – who were most detrimentally affected. Other regions had, for some time, been gradually adapting to the dictates of commercial agriculture, but until the late 1940s the western region manifested the demographic and economic characteristics of a peasant socio-cultural system (Hannan, 1979; Hannan and Hardiman, 1978). The poorest farmers in that region had the highest marriage and replacement rates in rural Ireland; their marriage and inheritance decisions were not governed by the economic evaluations that prevailed elsewhere. This distinctiveness disappeared in the 1950s when, in the course of massive depopulation through emigration, the region's population became a residual, post-peasant class, its members marginal in every sense: elderly, poor, geographically and socially isolated.

What impact did this process of marginalisation have on conflict and the efficacy of conflict management in major categories of relationships? A comparison of the picture of the rural community presented by Arensberg and Kimball for the 1930s with that offered by more recent ethnographers (Leyton, 1966; Messenger, 1968) and by Hannan's (1978; 1979) survey of farm families highlights the likely changes. These studies, while speaking most directly to rural areas in the west, indicate trends broadly applicable to the more prosperous farming regions of the east and midlands.

The most influential view of Irish peasant life, derived largely from Arensberg and Kimball's (1940) ethnography, emphasises consensus and co-operation to the virtual exclusion of conflict. A high potential for stress in family relationships is acknowledged, but it is countered by the presence of an effective system of stress management. The potential is understandable: relationships most prone to conflict, those involving property rights and authority, were solidly embedded in the family. Dependence of children on their parents – and particularly of sons upon their fathers – extended into late middle age. Recognising the latent violence, Synge (1907/1964) made the tension between generations the theme of *The Playboy of the Western World*, and thus marked patricide as the archetypical rural Irish murder; Gibbon (1973, p. 490) asserts that inter-generational conflict figures in nearly every serious fictional description of rural Ireland published in the past 50 years.

Similar distributions of stress among relationships were found by Leyton (1966) during the 1960s in a Northern Ireland village and by Messenger (1968) in a west of Ireland community. In both studies, the potential for conflict was judged to be high in relationships between relatives. But where the potential was greatest – among those related through the paternal line – overt conflict was rare. In general, conflict between relatives took the form of verbal arguments or the severance of contact; attempts to injure were confined to rare disputes between non-kin. Despite the potential for conflict in the traditional community, "it seemed possible to contain the inevitable tensions resulting from the very high rate of postponed adulthood, non-marriage, and the persistent subservience of women and older sons" (Hannan and Katsiaouni, 1977, p. 2). Conflict regulation in this view occurs at the level of the interdependent community through shared ideals for the conduct of interpersonal relationships, and at the family level through the possibilities for avoidance and withdrawal offered by extreme role differentiation. But such mechanisms of conflict regulation may only be viable in the insular traditional village.

The dependence of the rural economy on the fulfilment of mutual assistance obligations makes neighbourhood acquaintance a particularly significant relationship in rural areas. At the same time, the economic and symbolic importance attached to land proprietorship makes trespassing, rights of way, and grazing rights potent sources of contention between neighbours. Contrary to the claim that it is "occasional, superficial and unstructured" (Leyton, 1966, p. 541) it can be argued that acquaintanceship in rural areas (in contrast to urban areas) is likely to involve individuals as "whole persons", to use Simmel's (1923/1955, p. 44) phrase. Likewise, the proposal that stress and conflict are controlled by the "villagers' clear awareness of the consequences for group relations of open disputes between non-kin" (Leyton, 1966, p. 54) needs to be balanced by a recognition that the dissolution of the peasant·system reduced the effectiveness of shared ideals. While contact with strangers remained infrequent and disinterested, acquaintanceship was subject to considerable stress in marginal rural areas.

To derive a set of expectations as to patterns of conflict in rural Ireland during the 1950s is not then a straightforward matter. The inter-generational balance of the population was drastically altered by emigration – of farm children, only one-twentieth of the girls and one-fifth of the boys stayed in their native localities (Hannan and Katsiaouni, 1977, p. 26). But the very intrusion of change into a stagnant system acted to intensify the potential for conflict between the young who remained and the older generation who retained control over land and farming practices. Coser's (1970, p. 79) more general observation succintly expressed the tension involved:

> The breakdown of tradition creates in the young two seemingly contradictory expectations: the fear that the gradual advancement in the age hierarchy is put into question, and the hope that it is no longer necessary to wait the requisite number of years for the rewards of maturity.

In marginal rural areas, therefore, inter-generational homicide is expected to be strongly represented.

Within this larger picture, long-term adjustments to changing role expectations within families began in the 1950s to affect patterns of interspousal accommodation. Withdrawal and avoidance were no longer adequate since adherence to traditional role definitions would itself lead to alienation between spouses (Hannan and Katsiaouni, 1977; Hannan, 1978). Moreover, to the extent that institutionalisation of conflict regulation is difficult when one participant in the relationship maintains the old rules while the other honours the new, the management of conflict was less likely to be successful. Though the full impact of these changes would not be felt until the 1970s, during the earlier period a relatively high level of intra-generational family homicide is to be expected.

As was noted in Chapter 2, during the 1950s, the distinctive pattern of Irish rural to urban migration blunted the impact on cities of rural change. Emigration absorbed the bulk of those dislocated by farm mechanisation, while migrants to Irish cities, and in particular to the capital, were primarily drawn from the rural middle class. By the 1960s the locus of structural change had shifted decisively to urban areas. A policy of industrialisation initiated in 1958 transformed occupational structure and moved major institutional arrangements toward the pattern of the advanced capitalist societies. Changes in the distribution of conflict potential among relationships followed this momentum, and it was in the cities that the logic of these changes was worked out most completely. Industrialisation, like farm mechanisation, marginalised a large section of the labour force. Unskilled manual workers, whose position had always been tenuous, found themselves competing for a diminishing pool of available jobs. The safety valve of emigration deferred the full consequences for a time, but, increasingly, a social welfare poor, dependent on state transfer payments as their primary source of income, was formed.

More broadly, industrialisation accentuated changes incipient in the 1950s in the conflict potential of relationships. As property and authority became less exclusively linked to the family, an enlarged set of relationships – personal friends, neighbours, work or business acquaintances – developed a propensity for conflict. Further, the very density of urban population increases the frequency of casual interpersonal encounters. Acquaintanceship, which in traditional communities was a relationship between "whole persons", is increasingly defined by a coincidence of one or a few common interests or characteristics. A reciprocity of conflict potential and conflict control seems to exist in such relationships; but the more superficial the relationship the less institutionalised is the conflict.

Sociological or anthropological research on urban Ireland is sparse in contrast to that available for rural areas. Two studies, however, are directly relevant to the issues discussed here. The level of serious injury from interpersonal violence in urban areas during the 1970s is very low by international standards (Rottman, 1976). Nevertheless, O'Neill's (1971, pp. 487–488) observational research in a Dublin working class neighbourhood suggests that the characteristics of participants in such violent incidents as do occur conform to the pattern found elsewhere: they are young men of working class backgrounds. A high level of conflict potential is present, and frequently leads to violence, but conflict is largely confined to a highly institutionalised group context (O'Neill, 1971, pp. 485–486; 491–492). The possibility of serious injury being inflicted is therefore substantial only in the less frequent conflicts among strangers and slight acquaintances. For this reason urban homicide in the 1970s is expected to be predominantly intra-generational, the young victims and offenders sharing similar marginal backgrounds.

By the 1970s, the complexities involved in successfully maintaining family relationships in urban areas had greatly increased. In part this stems from an accentuation in urban centres of trends, identified as incipient in rural areas during the 1950s, that diversify the potential flashpoints for family conflict. Mistreatment, for example, of a wife by her husband is less likely to be passively endured, either by her or by sons and daughters; alliances between family members become more likely. An increased involvement of women in family conflict is implied, but the major consequence is that the ability to regulate conflict increasingly depends on a family's class position. Those in marginal structural locations are least equipped with the material and interpersonal resources needed to deal with the new complexities.

The diminution of the conflict potential within families through the transfer of property and authority relationships to other contexts, the changing content of the acquaintance relationship, and the increased contact among strangers are the clearest contrasts between the 1950s and the 1970s. It is expected that homicide will, as a result, shift from predominantly inter-generational to intra-generational. That expectation emerges when farmers in the west region are used to typify homicide in the 1950s and the marginal working class to typify homicide in the 1970s. In each period, the residents of the selected location were the most affected by structural change. However, differences between the two periods did not emerge through one set of structural pressures and relationships superseding another as conducive to homicide. Rather a gradual superimposition of new situations occurred. These new situations were mainly urban, for it was there that change in the 1960s and early 1970s was concentrated. In rural areas, though the process of accommodation to a transformed agricultural structure occurred over decades, the major dislocations were experienced in the 1950s. And if this is correct, then the contrast between the decades ought primarily to reflect emergent patterns of urban homicide.

These expectations will be tested using data on 169 homicides that occurred in 1951–60 and in 1970–74. Of those 169 victims, some were attacked by more than one offender, where the term "offender" denotes a person formally identified by the gardai as responsible for an offence. Given this study's preoccupation with the relationship between victims and offenders, it is necessary to allow for homicides with multiple offenders. This is accomplished by compiling the data for use in two formats – on the basis of victims and on the basis of offender-victim pairs. Curtis (1974) discusses the analytic rationale and implications of this approach, which allows for the use of either format according to the research question being considered. The 67 homicides during the 1950s involve 72 offender-victim pairs; the 102 homicides identified for the 1970s involve 127 such pairs. The proportion of multi-offender homicide is considerably greater in the 1970s.

Regional, urban/rural, occupational and relationship classifications, together with the contrast of the two time periods, form the working framework for the analysis. The data for the variables listed below were compiled from information supplied by the Garda Siochana from their files, supplemented, where necessary, from contemporary newspaper reports of incidents and legal proceedings (*The Irish Times*, various issues).

Region: four regions were derived primarily from the demographic studies cited above (Hannan, 1979; Hannan and Hardiman, 1978). As well as the contrasting east and west regions already discussed, there is a demographically intermediate South Region with prosperous farming areas, and a residual Midlands/Border Region, demographically and economically distinct. The accompanying map shows the composition of these regions.

Urban/Rural Context: four categories form an urban/rural dimension that ranges from "urban centres" to "villages, open country". The first category includes the five major urban centres: Dublin, Cork, Waterford, Limerick, and Galway. Cities over 10,000 in population form the next category along the dimension, followed by towns with populations between 500 and 9,999. All remaining areas are defined as "villages, open country".

Occupation: a five-category modified Hall-Jones scale was developed to allow both isolation of particular groups and comparability with the occupational data contained in the Census of Population. The five categories used in the analysis are: farmers and agricultural workers, white collar workers, routine non-manual occupations, skilled manual workers, unskilled and semi-skilled manual workers (including casual labourers).

REPUBLIC OF IRELAND: COMPOSITION OF REGIONS

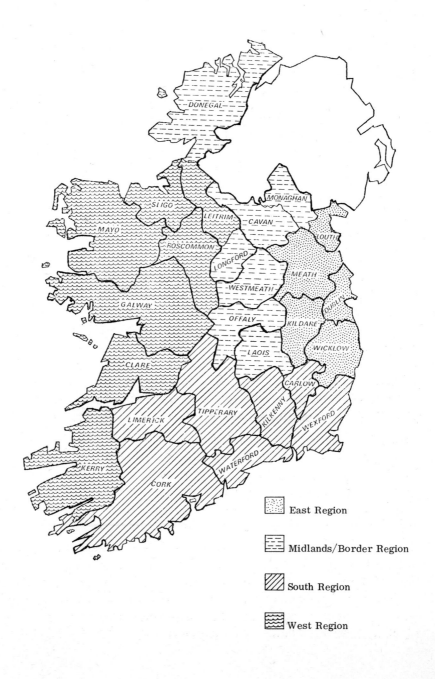

East Region

Midlands/Border Region

South Region

West Region

Relationship: four relationship categories – kin, spouse, acquaintance, stranger – are used. All relatives, other than spouses, are included in the first category. Acquaintanceship is broadly defined to comprise non-kin relationships of any duration.

Analysis

The first question addressed in the data analysis is the extent to which differences between the two decades can be identified. Table 20 assigns the homicides in each decade to the regional and urban/rural contexts in which they occurred, with the resulting distribution compared to that expected if the distribution were to correspond precisely to that of the general population. In the 1950s, expected and observed distributions coincide: the majority of both the population and the homicides were rural and the regional distribution of homicides mirrors that of the population. Comparisons are less straightforward in the 1970s. Homicides in that period under-represent rural areas and over-represent the urban centres, while more homicides occur in the east region and fewer in the west and south regions than a random distribution would predict. The prevalance of homicides of all types, therefore, is more clearly implicated in structural differences in the 1970s than in the 1950s, and the growth in incidence can be attributed to urban areas. However, chi square tests do not allow rejection of the null hypothesis that the observed frequencies of homicide are distributed in accordance with the population.

Table 21 examines the incidence of homicide by the four major categories of relationship. In the 1950s, 35.4 per cent of all homicides were within the family and 7.7 per cent involved people who could be described as strangers. The corresponding figures for the 1970s are 24.4 per cent and 23.5 per cent. The broadly defined category of "acquaintance" accounts for over one half of all homicide relationships in both periods. The differences are less marked when the homicide relationship is described on the basis of the sexes of the offender and of the victim. Table 22 shows a slight increase in the incidence of men killing other men and a comparable decrease of incidents in which men kill women. Men were held to be responsible for 91.3 per cent of all homicides in the 1950s and 93.5 per cent of all homicides in the 1970s; but incidents in which women killed men were more common in the 1970s than in the 1950s.

While Tables 21 and 22 contrast the two decades, the differences present within each period in the distribution of types of homicide among contexts are ignored. Thus, a second question must be asked before the impact of structural change can be assessed: to what extent do categories of relationship and the sex of victims and offenders differ between urban and rural areas? Given the small number of cases recorded during the 1950s, the use of percentages requires caution; both the percentages and the actual numbers will be given.

Table 20: *Expected and observed distributions of homicides by urban/rural and regional classifications*
(based on number of victims)

| Urban/Rural | 1950s | | 1970s | |
	Expected	Observed	Expected	Observed
	per cent	*per cent*	*per cent*	*per cent*
Urban centres	28.6	25.8	34.9	41.6
Cities	4.4	8.6	5.4	3.0
Towns	11.8	12.1	16.4	21.8
Villages	55.3	53.4	43.4	33.7
	100.0**	100.0	100.0	100.0
		(N = 58)		(N = 101)
	Chi square = 2.40		Chi square = 6.40*	

Region	Expected	Observed	Expected	Observed
	per cent	*per cent*	*per cent*	*per cent*
East	32.3	34.3	38.2	46.1
West	23.0	20.9	19.4	12.7
South	29.7	32.8	29.4	23.5
Midlands/border	15.0	12.0	13.0	17.7
	100.0	100.0	100.0	100.0
		(N = 67)		(N = 102)
	Chi square = 0.88		Chi square = 6.84*	

*Statistically significant at .10 level, 3 d.f. (.05 level $\geqslant$ 7.8; .10 level $\geqslant$ 6.3)
**Deviations from 100.0 per cent are due to rounding errors.

For the 1950s, of the 21 urban homicides – defined by combining the "urban centres" and the "cities" – one-third (7 of 21) were within families and 52.4 per cent (11 of 21) were between acquaintances. In the same period 34.2 per cent (13 of 38) of rural homicides were within families and 63.2 per cent (24 of 38) between acquaintances. For the 1970s, 18.2 per cent (10 of 54) of the urban homicides were within families and 47.3 per cent (26 of 54) among acquaintances. Rural homicides in the 1970s were within families in 29.7 per cent (19 of 64) of all identifiable victim-offender pairs and between acquaintances in 56.3 per cent (36 of 64) of all pairs.

Table 21: *Victim/offender relationships: 1950s and 1970s*
(based on victim/offender pairs)*

Relationship	1950s	1970s
	per cent	*per cent*
Kin	24.6	18.5
Spouse	10.8	5.9
Acquaintance	56.9	52.1
Stranger	7.7	23.5
	100.0	100.0
	(N = 65)	(N = 119)

*Rounding errors explains totals not equal to 100.0 per cent; the number of cases in a decade varies between tables according to data availability.

Table 22: *Sex of offender by sex of victim: 1950s and 1970s*
(based on victim/offender pairs)

Offender/Victim	1950s	1970s
	per cent	*per cent*
Male–Male	62.3	69.1
Male–Female	29.0	24.4
Female–Male	2.9	4.1
Female–Female	5.8	2.4
	100.0	100.0
	(N = 69)	(N = 123)

Family homicides, therefore, formed the same proportion of all homicides in urban and rural areas in the 1950s. By the 1970s that proportion had declined for both types of areas, but the more marked decline in urban areas results in a substantial urban/rural difference. In each period, the victim was the offender's spouse in seven of the homicide relationships. And in both periods six of those seven homicides were rural. The incidence of spouse killings was far greater in rural than in urban areas in both periods, and rural family homicides were concentrated in husband-wife relationships.

In the 1950s, a woman was the victim of 8 of 23 urban and 15 of 41 rural homicides – just under one-third in both cases. This contrasts with the situation in the 1970s when 31.9 per cent (22 of 69) of the rural, but only 21.1 per cent (12 of 57) of urban offender-victim pairs involved a female victim. In sum, differentiation among locations in the incidence of homicide and in the nature of the victim-offender relationship was less marked in the 1950s than in the 1970s.

The extent of differentiation in the ages of those identified as victims and offenders is the next issue. The average ages of victims and offenders in both periods are given separately in Table 23 for the major relationship, regional, urban-rural, and occupational categories. In the 1950s the age of the victim varies across categories while the average offender age is constant. Victims are considerably older, on average, in the west region, outside of the urban centres, and among farmers. The result is a clear pattern in those locations of inter-generational homicide. For example, in the west region the average age of victims (55.7 years) is higher and the average age of offenders (31.1 years) lower than in other regions. A low average victim age in the east region, in the urban centres, and among semi and unskilled manual workers makes intra-generational homicide characteristic of these locations. For the relationship categories being examined, distinctive average ages of victims make homicide appear to be predominantly intra-generational within families and inter-generational in other contexts.

Victims in the 1970s are older in the west region, in the rural areas, and among farmers, than in other locations: the pattern of inter-generational homicide persists. A less emphatic tendency to inter-generational homicide in other contexts is manifest in an overall trend toward younger offenders in the 1970s, and in an increase in the east region and in the urban areas in the average victim age. For example, the average victim age in the east region in the 1970s is 36.1 years; that of the offender is 25.8 years. While the use here of the label "inter-generational" is an overstatement, the clear pattern of *intra*-generational homicide found in the 1950s for those locations is no longer identifiable.

Given that the age structures of the four regions are not equivalent, the west region population being particularly weighted toward the elderly, the persuasiveness of the regional differences in victim ages, shown in Table 23, is contingent on the age structures of the respective regional sub-populations. In Table 24 the average age of victims is juxtaposed to that of the general population in each region and ratios are derived. This procedure confirms and clarifies the established pattern of regional differences. Not only are victims in the west region older than elsewhere, but the average victim age exceeds that of the population to a substantially greater extent than in other regions. The victim-population age ratios of 1.61 in the 1950s and 1.48 in the 1970s for the west region contrast markedly with those for the east region, where victim and population ages are nearly equivalent.

Table 23: *Average ages of victims and offenders (1950s and 1970s)*

	1950s		1970s	
	Victims	*Offenders*	*Victims*	*Offenders*
Relationship:				
1 Family	36.7	34.1	41.6	30.2
	(29.8/14)	(12.2/14)	(28.4/21)	(8.6/22)
2 Spouse	39.4	42.9	50.3	52.3
	(16.1/7)	(18.4/7)	(12.5/7)	(11.6/7)
3 Acquaintance	43.5	33.8	37.2	27.3
	(19.2/31)	(16.1/35)	(21.7/49)	(11.6/62)
4 Stranger	49.6	27.8	38.2	23.8
	(23.2/5)	(3.3/5)	(21.0/17)	(7.0/27)
Region:				
1 East	31.5	34.1	36.1	25.8
	(17.9/22)	(12.4/23)	(22.4/47)	(9.6/61)
2 West	55.7	31.1	52.8	30.1
	(19.6/13)	(15.6/14)	(24.3/13)	(17.0/14)
3 South	45.1	31.4	39.6	29.8
	(23.0/20)	(12.8/17)	(23.1/24)	(12.8/25)
4 Midlands/border	45.7	42.8	40.5	31.5
	(18.2/7)	(20.4/10)	(23.0/18)	(12.0/23)
Context:				
1 Urban centres	28.7	32.0	38.4	25.2
	(23.3/15)	(8.4/17)	(22.8/42)	(8.3/53)
2 Cities	50.4	38.2	37.0	20.3
	(29.0/5)	(19.3/5)	(26.1/3)	(2.5/3)
3 Towns	45.6	31.2	36.5	27.8
	(22.6/7)	(16.0/6)	(24.0/22)	(11.5/26)
4 Villages	47.7	36.4	43.2	33.0
	(17.0/29)	(16.7/30)	(23.4/34)	(14.7/40)
Occupation:				
1 Farming	51.5	36.7	49.8	35.8
	(15.3/24)	(17.2/24)	(22.7/20)	(15.6/17)
2 White Collar	39.9	45.2	44.2	30.1
	(25.7/7)	(10.5/5)	(24.3/10)	(9.5/7)
3 Non-Manual	37.4	32.3	42.0	33.3
	(27.7/8)	(15.2/6)	(23.1/23)	(15.3/14)
4 Skilled	39.0	36.5	27.7	28.2
	(19.7/3)	(12.2/6)	(18.3/16)	(9.5/24)
5 Semi/Unskilled	28.4	30.5	31.2	24.5
	(18.0/15)	(10.9/14)	(18.7/23)	(9.9/49)
Sex of Victim:				
1 Male	43.0	34.3	36.7	27.1
	(21.0/39)	(15.0/41)	(20.8/70)	(10.2/90)
2 Female	41.8	33.6	46.7	31.2
	(23.2/23)	(14.9/23)	(26.7/32)	(15.1/33)
Grand Mean:	42.5	34.1	39.8	28.2
	(21.6/62)	(14.9/64)	(23.2/102)	(11.8/123)

*Numbers in parentheses represent (standard deviation/number of cases).

Table 24: *Regional variation in victim age: ratios of average victim and average population ages*

| Region | 1950s | | | 1970s | | |
	Victim Average	Population Average	Ratio	Victim Average	Population Average	Ratio
East	31.5	31.4	1.00	36.1	30.9	1.17
West	55.7	34.7	1.61	52.8	35.6	1.48
South	45.1	33.6	1.34	39.6	33.0	1.20
Midlands/Border	45.7	34.0	1.34	40.5	34.3	1.18

Table 23 reveals regional, urban/rural, and occupational differences in the average ages of victims and offenders for both the 1950s and 1970s. But the complexities of differences in average ages, both within and between decades, revealed in Table 23 cannot be resolved without further analysis. It is necessary to examine how the various dimensions combine to affect victim and offender ages, and to consider the manner in which relationship categories are implicated in differences among structural location categories. Multiple regression using dummy variables is the method of analysis adopted. Formally, the issue is whether the mean age of offender and the mean age of victim vary signif~~~~~~~~~~~~~~~~~~~~~~~~~~~, ~~~~~~~~~~~~~~~~, ~~~~~~~~~~~, ~~~ ~~~~~~~~~~~~~ ~~~~~~~~~~~~.

A dummy variable is a category of a nominal or ordinal variable treated as a separate variable. In the present analysis, regional location will, therefore, be treated as four dummy variables. For each observation, the region in which the homicide occurred is assigned a value of one; the other three regions are assigned the value zero. In carrying out the analysis, one category is omitted: it forms the reference by which the metric (unstandardised) regression coefficients obtained for the other categories can be interpreted. For example, in Table 25 the "midlands/border region" category is omitted from the equations and the first column of the table indicates that, when the type of relationship between victim and offender is controlled for, the mean age of offenders in the east region is five years less than that for offenders in the midlands/border region. The coefficient is the years to be added to or subtracted from the reference category to derive the mean for the category at issue. The choice of omitted category is arbitrary.

Table 25 presents the additive effects on offender age of the four major independent variables: relationship, region, urban/rural context, and occupation. The results take the form of nine equations, run separately for each decade, using various combinations of the predictors. Each column represents an equation. In examining these equations, the main concerns are to identify the best predictors, examine their stability when used jointly with other predictors, and to find the overall predictive ability of the variables. For a period, the multiple regression equations predict the ages of offenders in *each* homicide, based on what is known about the location of the homicide, the relationship the victim had to the offender, and the occupational group of the offender. The metric coefficients in Table 25 therefore, can be interpreted as the *average* age of offenders in a particular category of an independent variable – say, for all homicides in the east region – controlling for all other independent variables entered into that particular equation.

Table 25: *Regression results: additive effects (metric coefficients) on the ages of offenders, 1950s and 1970s*

	1950s								
Relationship:									
1 Kin	7.5	8.0	6.0	3.7	6.6	8.2			
2 Spouse	13.6	15.1	11.5	8.2	14.0	15.1			
3 Acquaintance	4.6	7.6	4.5	1.6	6.1	6.9			
4 Stranger									
Region:									
1 East	−5.0			−14.7*			−14.1*		
2 West	−6.5			−12.4			−13.8		
3 South	−8.6			−16.8*			−18.4*		
4 Midlands/border									
Context:									
1 Urban centre		−5.1			−3.4			−6.5	
2 Cities		−0.8			2.7			−5.5	
3 Towns		−6.0			−6.9			−3.9	
4 Villages									
Occupation:									
1 Farming			5.8	5.2	3.5				6.3
2 White collar			12.4	14.4	13.3				13.8
3 Non-manual			−3.9	−2.4	−3.6				−4.6
4 Skilled manual			8.9	5.0	8.5				8.6
5 Semi/unskilled manual									
Constant	35.0	30.2	26.3	42.2	27.4	27.8	49.5	38.7	31.4
R²	.10	.10	.16	.27	.19	.06	.14	.04	.12
N	50	50	50	50	50	50	50	50	50

continued on next page

Table 25 *continued*.

	1970s								
Relationship:									
1 Kin	6.5*	7.4*	4.3	4.5	6.8*	6.5*			
2 Spouse	28.6*	30.2*	26.8*	26.7*	29.9*	28.6*			
3 Acquaintance	3.9	4.2	2.2	2.7	3.9	3.6			
4 Stranger									
Region:									
1 East	−7.5*				−6.3*		−7.2*		
2 West	−2.3				−3.2		−0.6		
3 South	−4.3				−3.6		−2.5		
4 Midlands/border									
Context:									
1 Urban centre		−7.3*				−6.4*		−8.8*	
2 Cities		−12.6*				−10.0*		−13.4	
3 Towns		−9.6*				−9.6*		−5.0	
4 Villages									
Occupation:									
1 Farming			9.6*	7.9*	3.1				11.0*
2 White collar			1.5	2.4	2.2				5.9
3 Non-manual			4.5	4.6	3.8				8.5*
4 Skilled manual			4.0	2.7	4.2				3.4
5 Semi/unskilled manual									
Constant	28.5	28.7	22.0	26.4	26.4	23.7	32.8	33.9	24.8
R^2	.35*	.40*	.36*	.39*	.42*	.29*	.07	.11*	.12*
N	108	108	108	108	108	108	108	108	108

*Denotes metric coefficients that exceed twice their standard error and R^2s statistically significant at .05 level.

Average offender age does not vary significantly among locations in the 1950s; in the 1970s, however, strong and consistent effects are readily identifiable. The only unambiguous association of offender age in the earlier period is with regional effects, but these do not differentiate the west region from the east or south regions. In contrast, in the 1970s all three locational variables and relationship are associated with offender age. In kinship, and especially spousal relationships, offenders are significantly older than elsewhere. The same is true when farmers are compared to non-farmers. Significantly, younger offenders are found in the east region and in urban areas generally during the 1970s. The explained variances in the 1950s, however, are not statistically significant, while those in the 1970s generally are.

Most of the coefficients remain stable across equations within each decade. The only real exception is the effect of farming in the 1970s – it does not remain significant when entered in the same equation as urban/rural context. Overall, the predictors appear to be relatively independent; each location variable has a moderate relationship to offender age, and in the 1970s particularly these effects cumulatively explain a substantial proportion of the variance in offender age.

In Table 26 which gives the additive effects for victim age, the predictive power of structural location is stronger in the 1950s than in the 1970s. The six equations shown for each decade do not include relationship as a predictor: the analysis is based on victims and where multiple offenders are involved it is not always possible to associate one type of relationship with a victim. For the 1950s, statistically significant effects are associated with urban/rural location, occupation and region. Victims in urban centres are younger than elsewhere and the farmers among the victims are older. While the occupational difference appears to be the stronger of the two effects, the urban/non-urban difference cannot be attributed solely to the situation of farmers. Together, the three regional categories explain a statistically significant 16 per cent of the variance in victim age, with victims in the west region considerably older than those elsewhere and victims in the east region younger. These effects are essentially duplicated in the 1970s, though in the later period only the effects of occupation are statistically significant.

The overall explained variance is satisfactory in both periods: for the 1950s urban/rural context and occupation explain 34 per cent of the variance in victim age, and in the 1970s region and occupation explain 21 per cent of the variance. However, while the predictors appear to be independent in the 1950s, they are less so in the 1970s where the dominance of the occupational category of farming over other effects is clear. Overall, the explained variances in the 1970s are unsatisfactory, with only two of the six equations having statistically significant R^2s.

All of the regression results presented thus far were based on additive effects. But if the effect of categories of relationship on the ages of victims and offenders varies with structural location, with a relationship category under more stress in some locations than others, it is necessary to consider interaction effects. To test for the presence of interaction, each category used in the preceding analysis was treated as a dichotomised variable. For example, the category "west region" was multiplied by each of the three relationship categories. The result was a multiple regression equation with seven predictors: the three relationship categories, the west region category, and the three multiplicative interaction terms. Then, the predictive ability of the equation was contrasted with that of an equation using only the four original dummy

Table 26: Regression results: additive (metric coefficients) on the ages of victims: 1950s and 1970s

	1950s						1970s					
Relationship:												
1 Kin												
2 Spouse												
3 Acquaintance												
4 Stranger												
Region:												
1 East	-2.8	-3.9	-9.1				-3.4	-4.9	-5.4			
2 West	15.9	10.8	14.5				18.7	13.0	16.0			
3 South	7.3	4.4	2.1				-0.9	-1.8	-1.8			
4 Midlands/border												
Context:												
1 Urban centre	-15.8*	-11.2	-19.6*				-2.8	3.7	-6.6			
2 Cities	-1.3	0.9	-14.8				-26.3	-5.5	-21.4			
3 Town	-3.2	10.5	-1.6				-4.2	3.2	-7.6			
4 Villages												
Occupation:												
1 Farming	20.0*	25.0*	25.4*				16.4*	21.8*	20.1*			
2 White collar	12.8	15.2	14.4				15.0	13.9	14.5			
3 Non-manual	7.4	15.4	11.9				12.6*	12.1	12.4			
4 Skilled manual	16.7	26.3	21.5				-1.8	-3.1	-2.0			
5 Semi/unskilled manual												
Constant	42.0	26.8	26.3	41.5	47.1	25.5	40.6	31.4	27.5	39.4	43.4	29.7
R^2	.25	.29*	.34*	.16*	.17*	.24*	.12	.21*	.16	.09	.03	.15*
N	52	52	52	52	52	52	91	91	91	91	91	91

*Denotes metric coefficients that exceed twice their standard error and R^2s statistically significant at .05 level

variables and an F-test was used to compare the two equations. Where the difference in explained variance is statistically significant, the correct specification of the association between type of relationship and the age variable is interactive: it depends on the structural location within which it occurs.

Tests for interaction were made separately for the two decades, using age of victim, age of offender, and the victim-offender age difference as the dependent variables. Only one test identified a statistically significant interaction effect: the effect of relationship on age differences in the 1950s varies across the regions. With the interaction terms included, the three relationship categories and the west region category explain 33.1 per cent of the variance in age difference; without the four interaction terms they explain 21.5 per cent of that variance. The difference is statistically significant at the .05 level ($F = 4.91$, d.f. $= 2,55$).

Discussion

In taking stock of the results, important differences emerge in the incidence and nature of homicide between the two decades and in each decade between locations. These differences, by and large, though by no means entirely, conform to the expected pattern.

A clear pattern of diversification of types of homicide emerged when the 1970s were contrasted with the 1950s. Regional, urban/rural, occupational, and relationship differences were slight within the 1950s, but marked within the 1970s. The only major exceptions to this were age differences and the incidence of spouse killings. The basic trends separating the two decades appear to be the diminishing importance of family homicide, an increasing proportion of homicides involving strangers, and a greater incidence of homicides in which women kill men. However, since rural homicide is essentially the same in both periods, the differences found between the 1950s and 1970s can be attributed to changes that occurred in urban areas.

Though age differences between victims and offenders do vary systematically in response to the major categories of relationship and to structural inequalities, the effect is not to create a clear shift from inter-generational to intra-generational homicide. Rather, marginal locations within each decade were marked by distinctive types of homicide. Two distinct patterns could be isolated for the 1950s. First, the expected pattern of inter-generational homicide emerged clearly for the west region and, more generally, for rural areas and farmers. The primacy of inter-generational homicide in those locations, however, cannot be attributed to conflict within families; family conflict was reflected in the homicide data, but largely in the form of spouse killings. Secondly, offender age did not vary across locations during the 1950s, but a distinctive pattern of intra-generational homicide was evident in the low average victim age associated with marginal urban locations.

The impact of marginal locations is still evident in the 1970s. Rural homicides, and those in the west region, replicate the patterns of the 1950s. The only clear distinction between decades for the rural areas is the increase in the average ages of victims and offenders involved in spouse killings, perhaps reflecting the problems experienced by traditional families adjusting to new expectations. That 35.7 per cent of rural homicides and 26.7 per cent of urban homicides had a female victim suggests the differences that have been created in the sources of conflict and the bases of conflict management for urban and rural areas. In the 1970s, no clear pattern of urban homicide can be selected; diversity is its defining characteristic. As would be expected, given the concentration of structural change in those locations during the years of rapid industrialisation, nearly all the changes in the nature of homicide between the 1950s and the 1970s can be attributed to urban centres. Certainly the increase in incidence was concentrated there: the number of urban homicides in the 1970s was four and a half times that in the 1950s; rural homicides over the same period registered a 2.5 fold increase. Thus, it does appear that structural change can be related to changing levels and patterns of offences against persons. The roots of the change, however, are to be found within relationships between persons, not in changing activities or in disorganisation. As relationships change, so do the potential for conflict and the potential for its peaceful resolution.

Chapter 7

Conclusions and Implications

In the last three chapters, a substantial number of charts and tables have been presented relating to Irish crime trends over the years 1951 to 1975. They were preceded by three chapters which, though largely free of numbers, discussed at a rather abstract level what factors, both within the society and inherent to the statistics themselves, might account for changes in the level and pattern of crime. In the present chapter, I hope to devise a vantage point somewhere between the abstract level with which the paper began and the specific statistical trends that were subsequently examined.

In seeking perspective, it may be useful to begin with a comment made a half century ago on the problem of crime in Ireland. The General Prisons Board in its report for 1925 issued a warning that will sound familiar to anyone who today regularly reads a newspaper:

> We have, within the last few years, to deal with an entirely new class of criminal, composed of half-educated youths who would appear to have escaped early from parental control. They have grown up in lawless habits, and the streets and the cinema have been the main sources of their moral education. Full of new and unsatisfied desires, these youths have been dazzled by sensational reports in newspapers of large sums of money obtained by organised robbery . . . Formerly a series of convictions for minor offences preceded offences of a grave nature. Now the first offender starts with the more serious form of crime (quoted in Molony, 1925–26, p. 183).

In the aftermath of the Civil War, a sense of a descent from previous standards of discipline and order is certainly understandable. But it is interesting to speculate on how today's assessments of the gravity of the problem of crime will read in fifty years time. I hope that on the basis of the preceding six chapters, it will be possible to make an assessment of the nature of the problem and its likely future course that will prove durable.

Three objectives were stated in the introductory chapter: to collate a valid set of indicators for the study of crime trends, to represent those trends in a manner that indicates the changes that have occurred since 1951 in the level and pattern of crime, and to interpret what took place. It was argued that if those objectives can be met, the precision and the usefulness of the current debate on crime would be enhanced.

Crime Indicators

The first objective was approached by a process of selection and annotation for the published statistics and the collection of supplementary information specifically for this study. Of these, selectivity in the choice of offence categories used is the most important. Nine indicators were chosen as minimising the traditional difficulties associated with crime statistics but still adequately reflecting the range of property crime. In my opinion, those indicators are reasonable representations of the actual change that occurred in the prevalence of crime.

From notes accompanying the annual statistics and from replies given by the gardai to my inquiries, it was possible to make some adjustments to the figures used and, more importantly, to establish the rules being followed in classifying and counting incidents. For aggregate statistics, further adjustments and improvements would be difficult. However, the absence of disaggregated crime statistics, reflecting the geographical distribution of offences, is a major limitation of the annual *Report on Crime*. The present study attempted to remedy that limitation for the period of greatest interest: 1964 and 1975. As a result, it was possible to compare the level of reported crime in three types of areas. A more refined breakdown of the statistics by city and by county would make a substantial improvement in the available data on crime. Such information can be obtained at present only when a question relating to a specific area has been asked in the Dáil.

The volume of reported crime that the gardai are at present processing each year precludes the abstraction of details that might indicate the diversity of the actions subsumed under each offence category. However, in terms of what we need to know about crime, both to understand its origins and to respond adequately to the social problem it represents, a plea for the availability of additional descriptive information cannot be avoided. An offence category such as burglary or larceny from shops comprises a multiplicity of targets, of monetary values, and of methods. Similarly, the category of assaults is comprised of interpersonal violence that occurs in many contexts and with a wide range of resulting injuries. Of the possible descriptive material that could be collected, there is probably a relatively small number of variables that the gardai themselves and others using the crime reports will view as essential. That information should be collected and published. If that is done, not only will the usefulness of the data on crime be far greater for both the gardai and for researchers – the statistics will then meaningfully relate to the issues on which public concern is based. At present, the crime statistics are of limited relevance to those issues.

The alternatives to police crime statistics – such as surveys of self-reported crime and of victimisation – will not overcome the limitations of the information already routinely published. In Chapter 3 a summary is given on the evaluation that can now be made on those alternatives. The enthusiasm with which survey estimates of crime were first greeted has not been sustained; the expense is prohibitive, the reliability of the resulting data is dubious, and there are few convincing studies in which the superiority of survey data to police statistics as indices of the level of crime were supported. Though survey data on crime may be desirable for specific purposes, there is no justification, in my opinion, for routinely collecting it.

If the garda crime statistics are to be the primary index of changes in criminal activity, how should it be used? Cautiously, is the most reasonable answer. However, this study does suggest some ground rules that should be implemented as part of the process of collecting and publishing crime statistics.

The most fundamental recommendation that can be made is that a handbook be prepared stating the rules operative in counting and classifying offences for all the categories listed in the *Report on Crime*. That the gardai do use a standard set of rules places the Irish crime statistics at a considerable advantage in comparison to what is available in most countries. If those rules are not themselves published, however, the advantage largely evaporates. The advantage disappears if modifications are introduced into the procedures that underlie the garda statistics without careful annotation in the relevant annual report. To summarise, the crime statistics should be placed on a sound bookkeeping basis.

The need for a more systematic approach to the publication of crime statistics is clearly evident in the substantial modifications made since 1975 in the format of the *Report on Crime*. For the most part, the changes are improvements, providing greater detail and shifting attention to the types of offences of interest to users of the report. But the modifications also introduce serious difficulties for anyone who wishes to compare trends before 1976 with what occurred in the remainder of the decade. It is essential that all changes in the compilation of the crime statistics be clearly signposted and fully explained. Where comparability with earlier reports is to be lost, consideration should be given to making available on request the information equivalent to what was previously published. At present, the *Report on Crime* is too easily misused.

If that is accomplished, then the minimum condition for taking the crime statistics seriously will have been fulfilled. But caution is still advisable. Above all, it is essential to avoid simplistic associations between changing crime levels and the effectiveness of the gardai. The resources and the efficiency of the Garda Siochana can also indirectly influence the level of reported crime in a manner that is both laudatory and likely to increase the crime rate. If the gardai are perceived by the public as capable of reacting to a citizen's claim that a crime took place, more crimes will be reported.

It follows that the crime statistics are not a particularly useful index with which to assess the benefits derived from increasing the number of gardai or the support facilities available to them. By being selective in the offence categories that are monitored, some of the difficulties can be eliminated and other sources of variation over time controlled, but the word caution must again be inserted.

The results shown in this study also suggest that a distinction is required between increases in the level of crime and increases in the seriousness of the resulting damage. Though more crime, of whatever variety, may be undesirable, it is possible that while crime has increased substantially, no real change has occurred in the type of crime that predominates. It is an important distinction. If, for example, a decision is to be made on the deployment of new gardai, or a re-distribution of gardai among districts and divisions, the type of crime in a locality may be a more useful guide than sheer offence levels. It is certainly more useful if decisions are being made on the desirable ratio between detectives and uniformed police.

To conclude, the garda crime statistics are of considerable use in the study of crime. It is a usefulness, however, that appears only after considerable effort has been expended. I hope that this paper has eased somewhat the work others will have to do in making use of the published information on crime.

The Growth of Crime

The trends in the nine crime indicators were examined over the 1951 to 1975 period for the entire nation and over the years 1964–75 separately for three types of areas. On the basis of the graphic, tabular, and statistical analysis of those trends, an assessment can be made of the dimensions of the change recorded in recent years.

The magnitude of the change dominates all the analyses. In Chapter 4, the litany of increases registered over the full 25 years, some as great as 29-fold, was depressing indeed. For all offences directed at acquiring property, with the exception of pedal cycle larceny and receiving stolen property, the 1975 level was at least five times what had appeared in the 1951 *Report on Crime*. The increase in both assault and homicide, included to represent violent offences against persons, was also substantial. That crime has become more prevalent since the 1950s appears to be indisputable.

That statement can be made with such confidence because alternative explanations of the increases, and particularly the possibility of changes within the gardai having artifically inflated the number of offences that become known, has little supporting evidence. The initial period of substantial annual increments in the statistics, the mid-1960s, was one of essentially declining garda manpower and an unchanging budget. In later years, the abrupt decline in detection rates poses an unanswered question, but it seems unlikely that the trends in known offences were seriously affected. This does not dismiss the possibility that part of the upward trend reflects a more rigorous definition of what incidents must be treated as "official" and thus entered into the statistics. But I do not see how such a change can account for the massive increases that were noted.

The only major break in the gloom is when attention shifts to the sophistication and organisation of criminal activities. If the average value of property stolen in burglaries can be taken as direct evidence of such changes, then crime is more prevalent today but not greatly different. The indirect evidence of the amount of increase in the number of recorded receiving stolen property offences leads to a similar conclusion. Both indicators recorded increases of less than two-fold over the full 25 years, a sharp contrast with the very substantial increases found for the other six property crime indicators.

The basic consistency of massive increases is paralleled by a consistent sequencing of the upward trends. For all offences except assault, the bulk of the growth in crime levels occurred subsequent to 1964. Throughout the 1950s and continuing into the early 1960s, the various indicators record cyclical fluctuations around an essentially horizontal trend line. Few actual increases were evident in the initial 13 years of the series. In all property offence indicators except that of pedal cycle larceny, a dramatic and apparently permanent break with that pattern occurs around 1964. Henceforth, the pace of increase is rapid, though for some indicators it tapers off by 1973 or 1974. A watershed clearly divides the trends in those indicators; the proper statistical specification for what took place is that of a structural break. Two trends rather than one are needed to accurately represent the changes. What occurred after 1964 had no precedent in the earlier years.

Two indicators just as clearly deviate from that basic pattern. The level of indictable assaults increased over the 25 years in a growth curve that began in the early 1950s. There is no basis for denoting the mid-1960s as marking an abrupt shift in the trend. Pedal cycle larceny in effect manifests no trend over the time-period. Rather, it has a cyclical pattern that persists throughout.

The perception that crime has become a more acute social problem, therefore, appears to be accurate, as does the belief that the bulk of that increase occurred quite recently. Indeed, it is reasonable to say that prior to the mid-1960s the levels of crime were such as to be almost imperceptible and no signs of the pending increases could be found. However, the use of crime statistics to establish the true level of an offence is considerably less reasonable than to use changing levels over time as indicators of trends.

Though the perception of the degree of change is verified by the evidence presented, the image of crime as predominantly an urban problem is not. The comparison of urban and rural crime trends in Chapter 5 emphasised the similarities rather than any clear differences. A predominance of urban trends in shaping what occurred at the national level is obvious only for two offences against property: housebreaking and larceny from vehicles. For the other indicators, the changing level crime did not differ greatly between Dublin, the four-cities, and the non-urban areas. Certainly, the presence of substantial increases in crime levels outside of the major cities is clear; it is also contrary to the basic assumptions underlying most discussions of crime in Ireland today. The theme of similarity across types of areas is further highlighted by the consistency in the sequencing of large increments over the 12-year period.

In one respect, crime is becoming a more serious problem in rural than in urban areas. The average value of property stolen in burglaries is expanding at a rate considerably in excess to that found for Dublin or the four-cities. Though crime may be more prevalent in cities, the difference in the degree of loss experienced, on average, from each offence that occurs elsewhere, suggests that as a problem crime lacks the urban focus that is often attributed to it.

As with the national crime trends, the alternative explanation of the impact of garda procedures and practices had to be considered. If gardai in different types of areas differ significantly in those respects, or if changes occurred in one area but not in another over the 12 years, then the comparisons become suspect. However, the consistency in detection rate trends across the three types of areas and the similarity in the detection rates themselves argue against such a suspicion being justified. As a measure of the magnitude of the problem of crime, the differences found for serious property crime – and especially burglary – tend to suggest that the situation is more precarious in rural than in urban areas. Again, this departs substantially from what is widely believed.

Taken together, the trends examined in Chapters 4 and 5 direct our attention toward a substantial transformation in the level and pattern of Irish crime, a transformation that was pervasive to the society as a whole. The consistency among the nine indicators examined is marked; given the variety of offences that they describe, and the length of the time-period considered, it is in many respects remarkable. It therefore seems reasonable to use those consistencies in the final section of this chapter as a basis for interpreting what took place and what is likely to take place in the near future.

Social Change and Crime

The trends summarised above support, by and large, the assertion that recent changes in the level and the pattern of crime in Ireland can most usefully be understood as responses to the specific social structural changes that originated around 1960. The comparisons shown between types of offences and between types of areas produced evidence of a substantial consistency that belies the view that the post-1964 increases took the form of a growing disorgansiation within the society. The timing of the transformation from cyclical fluctuation to a marked and sustained upward trend was generally consistent at the national level and the increases registered in urban and non-urban areas were essentially similar. On that evidence, it is reasonable to conclude that a watershed was reached, a departure from the level and pattern that had obtained since the early 1950s.

When national level trends covering the years 1951 to 1975 were examined, the extent of the transformation that occurred in the mid-1960s emerged clearly. For seven of the eight property offence indicators, for the inter-relationships among the indicators, and for the relationships the indicators have with measures of property availability and of economic conditions, the mid-1960s marks a watershed. The pattern of offence levels and of offence characteristics that had prevailed for several decades came to a conclusion around 1963, and was replaced by a new pattern. It seems reasonable to associate the emergent pattern with changes in Irish social structure that began in the late 1950s: the increase in crime was one offshoot of the adjustments being made to deep-seated structural change. The nature of the evidence being used precludes a formal rejection of social disorgansiation arguments, but here too it can be concluded that their applicability to Ireland is at best limited.

Urban/rural differences offer another concrete representation of the usefulness of social disorgansiation and structural perspectives. Had recent trends been such as to create marked disparities between types of areas, then social disorganisation explanations would appear appropriate. Such disparities were not marked, and while this does not in itself affirm the appropriateness of structural explanations, it does suggest that the latter approach is the more promising. For Ireland, a single transformation could be identified, largely ignoring boundaries between city and countryside, that between 1964 and 1975 significantly increased the level of crime, and, to a much lesser extent, altered the manner in which criminal activity is carried out.

This leads to a second and more difficult question: What components of structural change can be connected with the pattern of crime that emerged after the mid-1960s? Only a partial answer can be attempted in this paper. The amount of property available was used as one of many possible relevant aspects of structural change. When trends in availability of property were compared with those for offence levels and seriousness, however, a plausible connection did emerge. It is certainly sufficient to justify further research along the lines advocated in this paper, and some tentative conclusions. That belief is strengthened by the results obtained from the analysis of the effects from economic conditions on crime: cyclical variation in economic conditions have a minor relationship to changes in crime. Certainly that variation cannot explain the "break" in Irish crime trends.

The strongest support for a connection between structural change and crime levels was found for offence categories in which the most substantial changes took place over the 25 years in the amount and distribution of the property "at risk". Moreover, person offences – as represented by indictable assault – did not evince the same pattern of a clear break in levels of incidence; a continuous upward trend was present throughout the 25 years.

As I stated in Chapter 2, the difference between the social disorganisation and the structural perspectives can be too emphatic. Both associate substantial changes in a social structure with a higher incidence of crime. If preference is to be given to a structural approach, it is because it directs our attention to what is most important: the specific kinds of changes that Ireland experienced in the course of industrialising. A structural approach also has the advantage of eliminating the simple answer to the question of why social change should cause a growth in the level of crime, that of equating crime with disorder.

This summary of the monograph's conclusions can be read in the context of recent changes within criminology itself. Pessimism has of late come to be a defining trait of mainstream criminology: an imagery of despair pervades the recent work of many eminent criminologists. For example, Radzinowicz, as he surveys the mid-twentieth century increase in crime statistics that occurred in most countries, decries yet another country "succumbing to the plague" (1977, p. 7) and to the inevitable breaching of "the floodgates of juvenile delinquency" (ibid. p. 8) by the impact of the development process. Affluence and modernisation are his culprits, and, given the irreversibility of those processes, the future appears bleak indeed.

I have not sought to place Ireland within such an international context. Perhaps there is some world-historical process at work, of which Irish crime patterns are but one manifestation. But I suspect that is too convenient an answer, and also too simplistic. The diversity of change in the world today is considerable; whatever is shared among countries is balanced by the structural differences that are present. I am therefore left with a responsibility to provide my assessment of what the future course of crime in Ireland will be. If the trends presented here are a valid guide, then cautious optimism is the most reasonable basis on which to conclude. Placed in the context of the social changes Ireland experienced in the 1960s, the increases in crime are

perhaps less alarming than they would be viewed on their own. A transformation in the extent and pattern of crime occurred, one that is unlikely to be
repeated in the near future. It represented an adjustment to very substantial
changes in the social order. Now that the effects of those changes have been
largely absorbed within the system, though the level of crime may not
decrease, future increases may be more restrained than in the recent past.
Certainly statistical evidence for the late 1970s supports such an expectation.
Again, however, it is necessary to stress the limitations of the statistical
evidence. As an index of year to year changes, crime statistics are imprecise
and difficult to interpret. It is more sensible, I think, to view the statistical
trends in perspective, as achieved both by the use of interpretive frameworks
and a series of annual figures that cover a particular period.

REFERENCES

ARCHER, DANE and ROSEMARY GARTNER, 1976, "Violent Acts and Violent Times, A Comparative Approach to Postwar Homicide Rates", *American Sociological Review*, 41 (December): pp. 937–963.

ARENSBERG, C. and S. KIMBALL, 1940. *Family and Community in Ireland,* Boston: Harvard University Press.

BACON, PETER and MARTIN O'DONOGHUE, 1975. "The Economics of Crime in the Republic of Ireland," *The Economic and Social Review,* Vol. 7 (October): pp. 19–34.

BARTHOLOMEW, PAUL, C., 1971. *The Irish Judiciary,* Dublin: Institute of Public Administration.

BLAU, PETER, 1964. *Exchange and Power in Social Life,* New York: Wiley.

BLUMSTEIN, AIFRED, 1974. "Seriousness Weights in an Index of Crime", *American Sociological Review,* 39 (December): pp. 854–864.

BOGGS, SARAH, 1965. "Urban Crime Patterns," *American Sociological Review,* 30, pp. 899–908.

BOHANNAN, PAUL, 1960. "Patterns of Murder and Suicide", in P. Bohannan (ed.), *African Homicide and Suicide,* Princeton: Princeton University Press, pp. 230–266.

BOTTOMLEY, KEITH and CLIVE COLEMAN, 1976. "Criminal Statistics: The Police Role in Discovery and Detection of Crime", *International Journal of Criminology and Penology,* Vol. 4, No. 1, pp. 33–48.

BRODY, HUGH, 1973. *Inishkillane,* Harmondsworth: Penguin.

BROEKER, GALEN, 1970. *Rural Disorder and Police Reform in Ireland, 1812–36,* London: Routledge and Kegan Paul.

CENTRAL BANK OF IRELAND, 1977. *Data Bank of Annual Economic Time-Series, 1977,* Dublin: Research Department, Central Bank of Ireland.

CENTRAL STATISTICS OFFICE, 1973. *Census of Population of Ireland, Volume II: Ages and Conjugal Conditions,* Dublin: Stationery Office.

CHAPMAN, BRIAN, 1970. *Police State,* London: Macmillan.

CHOW, GREGORY, 1960. "Tests of Equality between Sets of Coefficients in Two Linear Regressions", *Econometrica,* 28 (July): pp. 591–605.

CLARK, JOHN P. and LARRY L. TIFFT, 1966. "Polygraph and Interview Validation of Self-reported Deviant Behaviour", *American Sociological Review,* 31 (August): pp. 516–523.

CLINARD, MARSHALL, B., 1942. "The Process of Urbanisation and Criminal Behavior", *American Journal of Sociology,* 48 (September).

CLINARD, MARSHALL, B., 1964. "The Relation of Urbanisation and Urbanism to Criminal Behaviour", in E. Burgess and D. Bogue (eds.), *Contributions to Urban Sociology,* Chicago: University of Chicago Press, pp. 541–558.

CLINARD, MARSHALL, B., 1978. *Cities with Little Crime: the Case of Switzerland,* London: Cambridge University Press.

CLINARD, MARSHALL, B. and DANIEL ABBOTT, 1973. *Crime in Developing Countries: A Comparative Perspective,* New York: John Wiley.

COHEN, ALBERT K., 1959. "The Study of Social Disorganisation and Deviant Behaviour," in R. Merton, L. Broom and L. Cottrell (eds.), *Sociology Today,* New York: Basic Books, pp. 461–484.

COHEN, LAWRENCE and MARCUS FELSON, 1979. "Social Change and Crime Rate Trends: a Routine Activities Approach", *American Sociological Review,* 44 (August): pp. 588–608.

COBB, RICHARD, 1978. *Death in Paris: 1795–1801,* Oxford: Oxford University Press.

COMMISSION ON THE GARDA SIOCHANA, 1970. *Report on Remuneration and Conditions of Service,* Dublin: Stationery Office.

COSER, LEWIS, 1970. *Continuities in the Study of Social Conflict,* New York: The Free Press.

CROTTY, R. D., 1966. *Irish Agricultural Production,* Cork: Cork University Press.

CURTIS, LYNN, 1974. *Criminal Violence,* Lexington, Mass.: Lexington Press

DEPARTMENT OF JUSTICE (Various Years). *Annual Report on Prisons*, Dublin: Stationery Office.

DEPARTMENTAL COMMITTEE ON CRIMINAL STATISTICS (PERKS COMMITTEE), 1967. *Report of the Departmental Committee on Criminal Statistics*, London: HMSO.

DOWNES, D. M., 1965. "Perks vs. the Criminal Statistics", *Criminal Law Review*, (January).

DURKHEIM, EMILE, 1933. *The Division of Labour in Society*, London: Collier-Macmillan (First Published in 1893).

DURKHEIM, EMILE, 1951. *Suicide: A Study in Sociology*, (Trans. J. Spaulding and G. Simpson), New York: Free Press (First published in 1897).

FERDINAND, T., 1967. "The Criminal Patterns of Boston since 1849", *American Journal of Sociology*. 73, pp. 84–99.

FOGARTY, M. P., 1973. *Irish Entrepreneurs Speak for Themselves*. Dublin: The Economic and Social Research Institute, Broadsheet No. 8.

GEARY, R. C. and J. G. HUGHES, 1970. *Internal Migration in Ireland* (with Appendix C. J. Gillman), Dublin: The Economic and Social Research Institute, Paper No. 55.

GERTH, HANS and C. WRIGHT MILLS, 1953. *Character and Social Structure*, New York: Harcourt, Brace and World.

GIBBON, PETER, 1973. "Arensberg and Kimball Revisited", *Economy and Society*, 2, (November): pp. 479–497.

GIBBS, JACK and MAYNARD ERICKSON, 1975. "Major Developments in the Sociological Study of Deviance", in A. Inkeles (ed.), *Annual Review of Sociology: 1975*, Palo Alto: Annual Reviews, pp. 21–43.

GIBBS, JACK and MAYNARD ERICKSON, 1976. "Crime Rates of American Cities in an Ecological Context", *American Journal of Sociology*, 82 (November): pp. 605–620.

GIDDENS, ANTHONY, 1971. *Capitalism and Modern Social Theory*, Cambridge: Cambridge University Press.

GIDDENS, ANTHONY, 1973. *The Class Structure of the Advanced Societies*, London: Hutchinson.

GOODE, WILLIAM, 1973, *Explorations in Social Theory*, New York: Oxford University Press.

GOLDFIELD, STEPHAN and RICHARD QUANDT, 1973. "The Estimation of Structural Shifts by Switching Regressions", *Annals of Economic and Social Measurement*, 2 (October): pp. 475–485.

GOULD, LEROY, 1971. "Crime and its Impact in an Affluent Society", in J. Douglas (ed.), *Crime and Justice in American Society*, Indianapolis: Bobbs Merrill, pp. 81–118.

HANNAN, DAMIAN, 1978. "Patterns of Spousal Accommodation and Conflict in Traditional and Modern Farm Families", *The Economic and Social Review*, Vol. 10 (October): pp. 61–84.

HANNAN, DAMIAN, 1979. *Displacement and Development Class, Kinship and Social Change in Irish Rural Communities*, Dublin: The Economic and Social Research Institute, Paper No. 96.

HANNAN, DAMIAN and LOUISE KATSIANOUNI, 1977. *Traditional Families? From Culturally Prescribed to Negotiated Roles in Farm Families*, Dublin: The Economic and Social Research Institute, Paper No. 87.

HANNAN, DAMIAN and NIAMH HARDIMAN, 1978. "Marriage rates and the changing social structure: Ireland 1871–1926", (Unpublished manuscript). Dublin: The Economic and Social Research Institute.

HANNAN, DAMIAN, D. ROTTMAN, N. HARDIMAN and M. WILEY, 1980. Class Structure and Income Inequality in Ireland. (Draft Manuscript), Dublin: The Economic and Social Research Institute.

HENRY, ANDREW F. and JAMES F. SHORT, 1954. *Suicide and Homicide*, Glencoe: Free Press.

HILLYARD, PATRICK, 1969. *The Nature and Extent of Crime in Ireland*, Unpublished Masters Thesis, University of Keele.

HINDELANG, MICHAEL, 1974. "The Uniform Crime Report Revisited". *Journal of Criminal Justice*, 2, pp. 1–17.

HINDELANG, MICHAEL, 1976. *Criminal Victimization in Eight American Cities,* Cambridge: Ballinger.

HINDESS, BARRY, 1973. *The Use of Official Statistics in Sociology.* London: Macmillan.

HIRSCHI, TRAVIS, 1972. *Causes of Delinquency.* Berkeley: University of California Press.

HOBSBAWM, E. J. and GEORGE RUDÉ, 1969. *Captain Swing,* Harmondsworth: Penguin.

HOOD ROGER and RICHARD SPARKS, 1970. *Key Issues in Criminology,* New York: McGraw-Hill.

HUGHES, J. G. and B. M. WALSH, 1980. *Internal Migration Flows in Ireland and their Determinants,* Dublin: The Economic and Social Research Institute, Paper No. 98.

HUTCHINSON, BERTRAM, 1969. *Social Status and Inter-Generational Social Mobility in Dublin,* Dublin: The Economic and Social Research Institute, Paper No. 48.

JACOBSON, ALVIN L., 1975. "Crime Trends in Southern and Non-Southern Cities: A Twenty Year Perspective", *Social Forces,* 54, (September): pp. 226–242.

KENNEDY, KIERAN and BRENDAN DOWLING, 1975. *Economic Growth in Ireland: The Experience since 1947.* Dublin: Gill and Macmillan in association with The Economic and Social Research Institute.

KROHN, MARVIN, 1978. "A Durkheimian Analysis of International Crime Rates", *Social Forces,* 57 (December): pp. 654–670.

LANE, ROGER, 1979. *Violent Death in the City: Suicide, Accident and Murder in 19th Century Philadelphia,* Cambridge: Harvard University Press.

LEWIS, GEORGE C., 1977. *Local Disturbances in Ireland,* Cork: Tower Books (First published in 1836).

LEYTON, E., 1966. "Conscious Models and Dispute Regulation in an Ulster Village", *Man,* 1, No. 4, pp. 534–542.

LODHI, A. Q. and C. TILLY, 1973. "Urbanisation, Crime and Collective Violence in 19th Century France", *American Journal of Sociology,* 79 (September): pp. 296–318.

LYNCH, PATRICK, 1966. "The Social Revolution that never was", in D. Williams (ed.), *The Irish Struggle, 1916-1926,* London: Routledge and Kegan Paul, pp. 41–54.

MANSFIELD, ROGER, LEROY C. GOULD and ZVI NAMENWIRTH, 1974. "A Socioeconomic Model for the Prediction of Societal Rates of Property Theft", *Social Forces,* 52 (June): pp. 462–472.

MARCEAU, JANE, 1977. *Class and Status in France,* Oxford: Oxford University Press.

McCARTHY, COLM and JUNE RYAN, 1976. "An Econometric Model of Television Ownership", *The Economic and Social Review,* Vol. 7, No. 3, pp. 265–277.

McCLINTOCK, F. H., 1963. *Crimes of Violence,* London: Macmillan.

McCLINTOCK, F. H., 1974. "Facts and Myths about the State of Crime", in R. Hood (ed.), *Crime, Criminology and Public Policy: Essays in Honour of Sir Leon Radzinowicz,* London: Heineman.

McDONALD, LYNN, 1976. *The Sociology of Law and Order,* Boulder: Westview Press.

MEENAN, JAMES, 1970. *The Irish Economy since 1922,* Liverpool: Liverpool University Press.

MERTON, ROBERT, 1957. *Social Theory and Social Structure* (Revised Edition). New York: Free Press.

MESSENGER, JOHN, C., 1968. "Types and Causes of Disputes in an Irish Community", *Eire-Ireland,* 3, No. 3, pp. 27–37.

MESSNER, STEVEN, 1978. "Income Inequality and Murder Rates: Some Cross-National Findings", Paper presented at the Annual Meetings of the American Sociological Association, San Francisco.

MILLS, C. WRIGHT, 1967. "The Professional Ideology of Social Pathologists", in I. L. Horowitz (ed.), *Power Politics and People: The Collected Essays of C. Wright Mills,* London: Oxford University Press. (First published in 1943).

MOLONY, SIR THOMAS, 1925–26. "The Probation of Offenders", *Journal of the Statistical and Social Inquiry Society of Ireland,* Vol. XV (continued): pp. 181–196.

MOORE, BARRINGTON, 1966. *Social Origins of Dictatorship and Democracy,* Harmondsworth: Penguin.

MORRIS, NORVAL and GORDON HAWKINS, 1970. *The Honest Politician's Guide to Crime Control*, Chicago: University of Chicago Press.

O'NEILL, CONOR, 1971. "The Social Functions of Violence in an Irish Urban Area", *The Economic and Social Review*, Vol. 2 (July): pp. 481–496.

Ó SÍOCHÁIN, P. A., 1977. *The Criminal Law of Ireland*, Dublin: Foilsiúcháin Dlí (*Sixth Edition*).

ORGANISATION FOR ECONOMIC CO-OPERATION AND DEVELOPMENT, 1976. *Data Sources for Social Indicators of Victimisation Suffered by Individuals*, Paris: OECD.

PARSONS, TALCOTT, 1949. *The Structure of Social Action: Second Edition*. New York: Free Press.

PIERCE, ALBERT, 1967. "The Economic Cycle and the Social Suicide Rate", *American Sociological Review*, 32 (June): pp. 457–462.

POGGI, GIANFRANCO, 1977. "The Constitutional State of the Nineteenth Century", *Sociology*, 11, (May): pp. 311–332.

PRESIDENT'S COMMISSION ON LAW ENFORCEMENT AND THE ADMINISTRATION OF JUSTICE, 1967. *Task Force Report: Crime and its Impact – An Assessment*, Washington D.C.: US Government Printing Office.

RADZINOWICZ, LEON and JOAN KING, 1977. *The Growth of Crime*, London: Hamish Hamilton.

REISS, ALBERT and DAVID J. BORDUA, 1967. "Environment and Organization: A Perspective on the Police" in D. Bordua (ed.), *The Police: Six Sociological Essays*, New York: John Wiley, pp. 25–55.

REPORT OF THE COMMISSIONER OF THE GARDA SIOCHANA ON CRIME (Various Years). Dublin: Stationery Office.

ROTTMAN, DAVID, B., 1976. "Crime Statistics and Crime Trends in the Republic of Ireland," Seminar Paper, Dublin: The Economic and Social Research Institute, 25th, November.

RUSSELL, MATHEW, 1964. "The Irish Delinquent in England", *Studies* 53 (Summer): pp. 136–148.

SCHWENDINGER, HERMAN and JULIA SCHWENDINGER, 1975. "Defenders of Order or Guardians of Human Rights?", in I. Taylor, P. Walton and J. Young (eds.), *Critical Criminology*, London: Routledge and Kegan Paul, pp. 113–146.

SHORTER, E. L. and C. TILLY, 1974. *Strikes in France, 1830 to 1968*, Cambridge: Cambridge University Press.

SIMMEL, GEORG, 1955. *Conflict and the Web of Group-Affiliations* (translated K. Wolff and R. Bendix) New York: The Free Press (First published in 1923).

SKOGAN, WESLEY, 1976. "The Victims of Crime: Some Material Findings", in A. Guenther (ed.), *Criminal Behavior in Social Systems*, Chicago: Rand McNally, pp. 131–148.

SMELSER, NEIL and SEYMOUR MARTIN LIPSET, 1966. "Social Strucutre, Mobility and Development", in N. Smelser and S. M. Lipset (eds.), *Social Structure and Mobility in Economic Development*, London: Routledge and Kegan Paul, pp. 1–50.

SNYDER, DAVID, 1975. "Institutional Setting and Industrial Conflict: Comparative Analyses of France, Italy and the United States," *American Sociological Review*, 40, (June): pp. 259–278.

SNYDER, DAVID, 1976. "Industrial Violence in Italy, 1878–1963," *American Journal of Sociology*, 82, (July): pp. 13–162.

SNYDER, DAVID, 1978. "Collective Violence", *Journal of Conflict Resolution*, 23, No. 3, pp. 499–534.

SNYDER, DAVID and CHARLES TILLY, 1972. "Hardship and Collective Violence in France, 1830–1960", *American Sociological Review*, 42 (October): pp. 105–123.

STEFFENSMEIER, DARRELL, 1978. "Crime and the Contemporary Woman: An Analysis of Changing Levels of Female Property Crime, 1960–75", *Social Forces*, 57 (December): pp. 566–584.

SYNGE, J. M. 1907/1964. "The Playboy of the Western World", *Classic Irish Drama*, Harmondsworth: Penguin Books, pp. 65–134.

TAYLOR, IAN, PAUL WALTON and JOCK YOUNG, 1973. *The New Criminology*, New York: Harper Torchbooks.

TAYLOR, IAN, PAUL WALTON and JOCK YOUNG, (eds.), 1975. *Critical Criminology*, London: Routledge and Kegan Paul.

THEIL, HENRI, 1971. *Principles of Econometrics*, New York: John Wiley.

TOBIAS J. J., 1972. *Crime and Industrial Society in the Nineteenth Century*, Harmondsworth: Penguin.

VIGDERHOUS, G., 1978. "Methodological Problems Confronting Cross-Cultural Criminological Research using Official Data", *Human Relations*, 31, (March): pp. 229–247.

VERKKO, V., 1953. "General Theoretical Viewpoints in Criminal Statistics Regarding Real Crime", in *Transactions of the Westermarck Society*, Copenhagen: Munksgaard, pp. 47–75.

VOLD, GEORGE, 1941. "Crime in City and Country Areas", *Annals of the American Academy of Political and Social Science*, 217, (September): pp. 38–45.

VOLD, GEORGE, 1958. *Theoretical Criminology*, New York: Oxford University Press.

WALKER, NIGEL, 1968. *Crime and Punishment in Britain*, Edinburgh: Edinburgh University Press.

WALSH, BRENDAN, 1968. *Some Irish Population Problems Reconsidered*, Dublin: The Economic and Social Research Institute, Paper No. 42.

WALSH, BRENDAN, 1974. "Expectations, Information and Human Migration: Specifying an Econometric Model of Irish Migration to Britain", *Journal of Regional Science*, 14, No. 1, pp. 107–120.

WALSH, BRENDAN, 1978. "Unemployment Compensation and the Rate of Unemployment: the Irish Experience", in H. Grubel and M. Walker (eds.), *Unemployment Insurance: Global Evidence of its Effects on Unemployment*, Vancouver: The Fraser Institute.

WEBB, ALVIN, L., 1972. "Crime and the Division of Labor", *American Journal of Sociology*, 78 (November): pp. 643–656.

WILLIAMS, DESMOND, 1966. "The Summing Up", in D. Williams (ed.), *The Irish Struggle, 1916–1926*, London: Routledge and Kegan Paul, pp. 183–193.

WOLFGANG, MARVIN, E. and F. FERRACUTI, 1967. *The Subculture of Violence*, London: Methuen.

WOOD, ARTHUR, 1961/1967. "Murder and other Deviance in Ceylon" in M. Wolfgang (ed.), *Studies in Homicide*, New York: Harper and Row, pp. 238–252.

ZIMRING, FRANKLIN, 1972. "The Medium is the Message: Firearm Caliber as a Determinant of Death from Assault", *Journal of Legal Studies*, 1, pp. 97–123.

THE ECONOMIC AND SOCIAL RESEARCH INSTITUTE

Books:
Economic Growth in Ireland: The Experience Since 1947
Kieran A. Kennedy and Brendan Dowling
Irish Economic Policy: A Review of Major Issues
Staff Members of ESRI (eds. B. R. Dowling and J. Durkan)

Policy Research Series:
1. *Regional Policy and the Full-Employment Target*   M. Ross and B. Walsh
2. *Energy Demand in Ireland, Projections and Policy Issues*   S. Scott

Broadsheet Series:
1. *Dental Services in Ireland*   P. R. Kaim-Caudle
2. *We Can Stop Rising Prices*   M. P. Fogarty
3. *Pharmaceutical Services in Ireland*   P. R. Kaim-Caudle
    assisted by Annette O'Toole and Kathleen O'Donoghue
4. *Ophthalmic Services in Ireland*   P. R. Kaim-Caudle
    assisted by Kathleen O'Donoghue and Annette O'Toole
5. *Irish Pensions Schemes, 1969*   P. R. Kaim-Caudle and J. G. Byrne
    assisted by Annette O'Toole
6. *The Social Science Percentage Nuisance*   R. C. Geary
7. *Poverty in Ireland: Research Priorities*   Brendan M. Walsh
8. *Irish Entrepreneurs Speak for Themselves*   M. P. Fogarty
9. *Martial Desertion in Dublin: an exploratory study*   Kathleen O'Higgins
10. *Equalization of Opportunity in Ireland: Statistical Aspects*
    R. C. Geary and F. S. Ó Muircheartaigh
11. *Public Social Expenditure in Ireland,*   Finola Kennedy
12. *Problems in Economic Planning and Policy Formation in Ireland, 1958–1974*
    Desmond Norton
13. *Crisis in the Cattle Industry*   R. O'Connor and P. Keogh
14. *A Study of Schemes for the Relief of Unemployment in Ireland*
    R. C. Geary and M. Dempsey
    with Appendix   E. Costa
15. *Dublin Simon Community, 1971–1976: an Exploration*   Ian Hart
16. *Aspects of the Swedish Economy and their relevance to Ireland*
    Robert O'Connor, Eoin O'Malley and Anthony Foley
17. *The Irish Housing System: A Critical Overview*   T. J. Baker and L. M. O'Brien
18. *The Irish Itinerants: Some Demographic, Economic and Educational Aspects*
    M. Dempsey and R. C. Geary
19. *A study of Industrial Workers Co-operatives*   Robert O'Connor and Philip Kelly
20. *Drinking in Ireland: A Review of Trends in Alcohol Consumption, Alcohol Related Problems and Policies towards Alcohol*   Brendan M. Walsh

General Research Series
1. *The Ownership of Personal Property in Ireland*   Edward Nevin
2. *Short-Term Economic Forecasting and its Application in Ireland*   Alfred Kuehn
3. *The Irish Tariff and The E.E.C.: A Factual Survey*   Edward Nevin
4. *Demand Relationships for Ireland*   C. E. V. Leser
5. *Local Government Finance in Ireland: A Preliminary Survey*   David Walker
6. *Prospects of the Irish Economy in 1962*   Alfred Kuehn
7. *The Irish Woollen and Worsted Industry, 1946–59: A Study in Statistical Method*
    R. C. Geary
8. *The Allocation of Public Funds for Social Development*   David Walker

General Research Series—*continued*

9. *The Irish Price Level: A Comparative Study* — Edward Nevin
10. *Inland Transport in Ireland: A Factual Survey* — D. J. Reynolds
11. *Public Debt and Economic Development* — Edward Nevin
12. *Wages in Ireland, 1946–62* — Edward Nevin
13. *Road Transport: The Problems and Prospects in Ireland* — D. J. Reynolds
14. *Imports and Economic Growth in Ireland, 1947–61* — C. E. V. Leser
15. *The Irish Economy in 1962 and 1963* — C. E. V. Leser
16. *Irish County Incomes in 1960* — E. A. Attwood and R. C. Geary
17. *The Capital Stock of Irish Industry* — Edward Nevin
18. *Local Government Finance and County Incomes* — David Walker
19. *Industrial Relations in Ireland: The Background* — David O'Mahony
20. *Social Security in Ireland and Western Europe* — P. R. Kaim-Caudle
21. *The Irish Economy in 1963 and 1964* — C. E. V. Leser
22. *The Cost Structure of Irish Industry 1950–60* — Edward Nevin
23. *A Further Analysis of Irish Household Budget Data, 1951–1952* — C. E. V. Leser
24. *Economic Aspects of Industrial Relations* — David O'Mahony
25. *Psychological Barriers to Economic Achievement* — P. Pentony
26. *Seasonality in Irish Economic Statistics* — C. E. V. Leser
27. *The Irish Economy in 1964 and 1965* — C. E. V. Leser
28. *Housing in Ireland: Some Economic Aspects* — P. R. Kaim-Caudle
29. *A Statistical Study of Wages, Prices and Employment in the Irish Manufacturing Sector* — C. St. J. O'Herlihy
30. *Fuel and Power in Ireland: Part I. Energy Consumption in 1970* — J. L. Booth
31. *Determinants of Wage Inflation in Ireland* — Keith Cowling
32. *Regional Employment Patterns in the Republic of Ireland* — T. J. Baker
33. *The Irish Economy in 1966* — The Staff of The Economic Research Institute
34. *Fuel and Power in Ireland: Part II. Electricity and Turf* — J. L. Booth
35. *Fuel and Power in Ireland: Part III. International and Temporal Aspects of Energy Consumption* — J. L. Booth
36. *Institutional Aspects of Commercial and Central Banking in Ireland* — John Hein
37. *Fuel and Power in Ireland: Part IV. Sources and Uses of Energy* — J. L. Booth
38. *A Study of Imports* — C. E. V. Leser
39. *The Irish Economy in 1967* — The Staff of The Economic and Social Research Institute
40. *Some Aspects of Price Inflation in Ireland* — R. C. Geary and J. L. Pratschke
41. *A Medium Term Planning Model for Ireland* — David Simpson
42. *Some Irish Population Problems Reconsidered* — Brendan M. Walsh
43. *The Irish Brain Drain* — Richard Lynn
44. *A Method of Estimating the Stock of Capital in Northern Ireland Manufacturing Industry: Limitations and Applications* — C. W. Jefferson
45. *An Input-Output Analysis of the Agricultural Sector of the Irish Economy in 1964* — R. O'Connor with M. Breslin
46. *The Implications for Cattle Producers of Seasonal Price Fluctuations* — R. O'Connor
47. *Transport in the Developing Economy of Ireland* — John Blackwell
48. *Social Status and Inter-Generational Social Mobility in Dublin* — Bertram Hutchinson
49. *Personal Incomes by County, 1965* — Miceal Ross
50. *Income-Expenditure Relations in Ireland, 1965–1966* — John L. Pratschke
51. *Costs and Prices in Transportable Goods Industries* — W. Black, J. V. Simpson, D. G. Slattery
52. *Certain Aspects of Non-Agricultural Unemployment in Ireland* — R. C. Geary and J. G. Hughes

General Research Series—*continued*

53. *A Study of Demand Elasticities for Irish Imports*   Dermot McAleese
54. *Internal Migration in Ireland*   R. C. Geary and J. G. Hughes
    with Appendix   C. J. Gillman
55. *Religion and Demographic Behaviour in Ireland*   B. M. Walsh
    with Appendix   R. C. Geary and J. G. Hughes
56. *Views on Pay Increases, Fringe Benefits and Low Pay*
    H. Behrend, A. Knowles and J. Davies
57. *Views on Income Differentials and the Economic Situation*
    H. Behrend, A. Knowles and J. Davies
58. *Computers in Ireland*   F. G. Foster
59. *National Differences in Anxiety*   Richard Lynn
60. *Capital Statistics for Irish Manufacturing Industry*   C. W. Jefferson
61. *Rural Household Budget–Feasibility Study*   Sile Sheehy and R. O'Connor
62. *Effective Tariffs and the Structure of Industrial Protection in Ireland*
    Dermot McAleese
63. *Methodology of Personal Income Estimation by County*   Miceal Ross
64. *Further Data on County Incomes in the Sixties*   Miceal Ross
65. *The Functional Distribution of Income in Ireland, 1938–70*   J. G. Hughes
66. *Irish Input-Output Structures, 1964 and 1968*   E. W. Henry
67. *Social Status in Dublin: Marriage, Mobility and First Employment*
    Bertram Hutchinson
68. *An Economic Evaluation of Irish Salmon Fishing, I: The Visiting Anglers*
    R. O'Connor and B. J. Whelan
69. *Women and Employment in Ireland: Results of a National Survey*
    Brendan M. Walsh assisted by Annette O'Toole
70. *Irish Manufactured Imports from the UK in the Sixties: The Effects of AIFTA*
    Dermot McAleese and John Martin
71. *Alphabetical Voting: A Study of the 1973 General Election in the Republic of Ireland*
    Christopher Robson and Brendan M. Walsh
72. *A Study of the Irish Cattle and Beef Industries*
    Terence J. Baker, Robert O'Connor and Rory Dunne
73. *Regional Employment Patterns in Northern Ireland*
    William Black and Clifford W. Jefferson
74. *Irish Full Employment Structures, 1968 and 1975*   E. W. Henry
75. *An Economic Evaluation of Irish Salmon Fishing II: The Irish Anglers*
    R. O'Connor, B. J. Whelan, and A. McCashin
76. *Factors Relating to Reconviction among Young Dublin Probationers*   Ian Hart
77. *The Structure of Unemployment in Ireland, 1954–1972*   Brendan M. Walsh
78. *An Economic Evaluation of Irish Salmon Fishing, III: The Commercial Fishermen*
    B. J. Whelan, R. O'Connor, and A. McCashin
79. *Wage Inflation and Wage Leadership*
    W. E. J. McCarthy, J. F. O'Brien and V. G. Dowd
80. *An Econometric Study of the Irish Postal Services*   Peter Neary
81. *Employment Relationships in Irish Counties*   Terence J. Baker and Miceal Ross
82. *Irish Input-Output Income Multipliers 1964 and 1968*
    J. R. Copeland and E. W. Henry
83. *A Study of the Structure and Determinants of the Behavioural Component of Social Attitudes in Ireland*   E. E. Davis
84. *Economic Aspects of Local Authority Expenditure and Finance*
    J. R. Copeland and Brendan M. Walsh
85. *Population Growth and other Statistics of Middle-sized Irish Towns*
    D. Curtin, R. C. Geary, T. A. Grimes and B. Menton

General Research Series—*continued*

86. *The Income Sensitivity of the Personal Income Tax Base in Ireland, 1947–1972*
Brendan R. Dowling

87. *Traditional Families? From Culturally Prescribed to Negotiated Roles in Farm Families*   Damian F. Hannan and Louise Katsiaouni

88. *An Irish Personality Differential: A Technique for Measuring Affective and Cognitive Dimensions of Attitudes Towards Persons*   E. E. Davis and Mary O'Neill

89. *Redundancy and Re-Employment in Ireland*
Brendan J. Whelan and Brendan M. Walsh

90. *A National Model of Fuel Allocation—A Prototype*   E. W. Henry and S. Scott

91. *A Linear Programming Model for Irish Agriculture*
Robert O'Connor, Miceal Ross and Michael Behan

92. *Irish Educational Expenditures—Past, Present and Future*   A. Dale Tussing

93. *The Working and Living Conditions of Civil Service Typists*
Nóirín O'Broin and Gillian Farren

94. *Irish Public Debt*   Richard Bruton

95. *Output and Employment in the Irish Food Industry to 1990*
A. D. O'Rourke and T. P. McStay

96. *Displacement and Development: Class, Kinship and Social Change in Irish Rural Communities*   Damian F. Hannan

97. *Attitudes in the Republic of Ireland relevant to the Northern Ireland Problem: Vol. I: Descriptive Analysis and Some Comparisons with Attitudes in Northern Ireland and Great Britain.*
E. E. Davis and R. Sinnott

98. *Internal Migration Flows in Ireland and their Determinants*
J. G. Hughes and B. M. Walsh

99. *Irish Input–Output Structures, 1976*   E. W. Henry

100. *Development of Irish Sea Fishing Industry and its Regional Implications*
R. O'Connor, J. A. Crutchfield, B. J. Whelan and K. E. Mellon

101. *Employment Conditions and Job Satisfaction: The Distribution, Perception and Evaluation of Job Rewards*
Christopher T. Whelan

102. *Crime in the Republic of Ireland: Statistical Trends and their Interpretation.*
David B. Rottman